AF553589

# ISSUES
# IN
# SCHOOL CURRICULUM

*By*

**Dr. Marlow Ediger**

*Professor Emeritus*
*Division of Education*
*Truman State University*
*P.O. Box 417, 201 W, 22nd St*
*North Netwon KS 67117*
*United States of America*

**Dr. Digumarti Bhaskara Rao**

*M.Sc., M.A., M.A., M.Ed., Ph.D.*
*Reader*
*R.V.R. College of Education*
*Srinivasa Nagar Colony*
*Guntur–522 006*
*&*
*Member*
*Board of Studies in Education*
*Acharya Nagarjuna University*
*Nagarjuna Nagar*
*Andhra Pradesh*
*(India)*

**DISCOVERY PUBLISHING HOUSE**
**NEW DELHI-110002**

Reprinted - 2018

First Published - 2006

ISBN: 978-81-8356-052-8



**Issues in School Curriculum**

*Published by:*

DISCOVERY PUBLISHING HOUSE PVT. LTD.

4383/4B, Ansari Road, Darya Ganj

New Delhi-110 002 (India)

*Phone*: +91-11-23279245, 43596064-65

*Fax*: +91-11-23253475

*E-mail*: discoverypublishinghouse@gmail.com

sales@discoverypublishinggroup.com

*web*: www.discoverypublishinggroup.com

*Printed at:*

Infinity Imaging Systems

Delhi

*Dedicated*
*To*

**Mr. Jelli Prasad**
*Founder and Correspondent*
*Andhra Kesari College of Education, Ongole*

**Mr. Gona Aseervadam**
*Founder and Correspondent*
*St. Paul's College of Education, Giddalur*

**Mr. M.A. Ahmad**
*Secretary and Correspondent*
*Al-Momin College of Education, Podili*

**Mr. Divi Ramesh**
*Secretary and Correspondent*
*Vivekananda College of Education, Kandukur*
*Annie Besant College of Education, Kandukur*
*Priyanka College of Education, Ongole*
*Andhra Pradesh*

# Preface

Curriculum is the soul of the process of education, heart of the educational institution and mind of the course. It is the sole tool in the hands of the teacher to mould the students according to the aims and objectives of education.

Curriculum is always in the making, being more in the nature of a process than a finished product. It informs concerned people what to teach before the consideration of the strategies of teaching. It is futile to talk 'how' and 'when' to teach without first deciding 'what' to teach.

Curriculum is very much dependent on the determination of educational directions, the choice of principles and procedures for selecting and ordering the potential experiences comprising the institutional programme, the selection of a pattern of curriculum organisation, and the procedures by which changes in the curriculum can be made. These four significant dimensions are essentially to be considered when one talks about curriculum.

Curriculum issues, hence, need a careful attention for the effective transaction of curriculum in the classrooms. This book "Issues in School Curriculum" discusses in detail various issues concerned to school curriculum. This book will be of great interest and use to curriculum specialists, school administrators and subject teachers.

**Bhaskara Rao**

**Sai Soudha**
*D-43, S.V.N. Colony*
*Guntur, 522 006*
*A.P. (India)*

## Contents

# Philosophy of Education in the Curriculum

Many decisions made in the curriculum of life are philosophical. Few choices are made empirically. Thus, in the school/class setting, teachers and supervisors need to choose from among the following which are quite opposite from each other:

1. programmed learning versus learning centres and open space education;
2. basal readers versus an individualised reading programme;
3. measurably stated objectives versus general goals in teaching learners;
4. teacher choice versus rather heavy learner input in determining objectives, learning activities, and evaluation procedures;
5. a textbook and workbook framework in teaching as compared to developing units of study utilising a variety of media and materials.

It is quite obvious that empirical objectives means can not be utilised solely in selecting objectives, learning activities, and evaluation procedures.

## Experimentalism in Education

Experimentalists believe that one can only know what is experienced. One presently experiences the here and the now.

The human being cannot experience the future. But, one reconstructs past learnings to harmonise with the present.

Change is a key concept, according to experimentalists. Scenes and situations in society are not stable nor static. New inventions, technology, and ideas are continually with us. With change in society, new problems arise. Old solutions to the identified problems, in general, do not work. Thus, new data needs gathering in answer to the identified problem. After adequate data or information has been attained, a hypothesis or answer to the identified problem must be generated. The hypothesis is tested in action and revised, if necessary learners then need to develop skills in problem solving. Each person in the here and now has problems. These need to be identified and solved.

Experimentalists do not believe in absolute knowledge. Knowledge changes in terms of relevancy, accuracy and usefulness. New knowledge is needed to offer solutions in problem-solving situations. Formalism, rigidity, and dogmatism are three concepts which experimentalists reject in problem-solving situations. Knowledge then is rather tentative, flexible, and subject to change. School and society do not reflect stability but change, openess, and newness. John Dewey wrote the following:

The nature of experience can be understood only by noting that it includes an active and a passive element peculiarly combined. On the active hand, experience is trying—a meaning which is made explicit in the connected term experiment. On the passive, it is undergoing. When we experience something we act upon it, we do something with it; then we suffer or undergo the consequences. We do something to the thing and then it does something to us in return: such as the peculiar combination. The connection of these two phases of experience measures the fruitfulness or value of the experience. More activity does not constitute experience. It is dispersive, centrifugal, dissipating. Experience as trying involves change, but change is meaningless transition unless it is consciously connected with the return wave of consequences which flow from it. When an activity is continued into the undergoing of consequences, when the change made by action is reflected back into a change made in us, the more flux is loaded with the significance. We learn something.

Experimentalists look at the consequences of an act rather than *a priori* statements or first principles. Thus, if a choice is to be made or a hypothesis to be tested, which consequences might accrue? There are no absolutes that one may cling to in the making of decisions. The ultimate decision made is openended. However, the end result should be that identified problems are solved. A change then results in moving away from what is to what should be. A believer in *a priori* statements believes that prior to any deed or act, universal ideals exist in leading one to make appropriate choices in school and in society. Opposite of *a priori* philosophies, the experimentalist looks at the consequences involved if one or several paths of action are followed as compared to other possible deeds or acts.

Experimentalists believe that the school curriculum should be integrated and not separated from society. Too frequently, the school is an isolated institution from the larger societal arena. Rather, what is relevant and desirable in society must become inherent in the curriculum of the school. Pertaining to the school as special environment, John Dewey wrote:

Hence a special mode of social intercourse is instituted, the school, to care for such matters.

This mode of association has three functions sufficiently specific, as compared with ordinary associations of life, to be noted. First, a complex civilization is too complex to be assimilated piecemeal, in a gradual and graded way. The relationships of our present social life are so numerous and so interwoven that a child placed in the most favourable position could not readily share in many of the most important of them. Not sharing in them, their meaning would not be communicated to him, would not become a part of the forest. Business, politics, art, science, religion, would make all at once a clamor for attention; confusion would be the outcome. The first office of the social organ we call the school is to provide a simplified environment. It selects the futures which are fairly fundamental and capable of being responded to by the young. Then it establishes a progressive order, using the factors first acquired as means of gaining insight into what is more complicated.

In society, group action is involved in identifying and attempting to solve problems. In the school setting also, learners in committees need to select and solve relevant problems. A miniature society is then in evidence. Dualisms need to be avoided, such as separating school from society, or learner interest from effort. If learners perceive interest in learning, they will put forth effort and reveal purpose in ongoing units of study. The learner must not be separated from the curriculum.

Morris and Pai wrote the following pertaining to experience involving ultimate reality of experimentalism:

Experience is the ultimate ground for human existence. It is both the originator and the supreme court of whatever we do or say. To put it bluntly once again, whatever reality it is what we say it is, and what we say it is founded in ordinary experience. Experience is as close as we can get to the "name" of reality. As exasperatingly non-substantive as this may be, it is the best we can do.

Knowing, then, must take on a quite different notation in this philosophy, for we are immediately confronted by the necessity to settle for something much less than fixed and permanent truth as the end point of our epistemological labours. Since our reality is characterised by flux and movement and change, certainly our knowledge cannot be otherwise. We must therefore initially retrain ourselves to recognise that whatever knowledge is possible is temporary and tentative in character. In our conception of truth (knowledge) is ultimately "at the mercy of phenomena" as we experience them, as Dingle has said, then we must be willing to alter our truth and our knowledge as new and variable phenomena come into view.

## A. Values, Ethics, and Experimentalism

Experimentalists definitely do not advocate absolutes in the values domain. Values change in time and place. They are applicable within a contextual situation. Values are tested in society and revised, if need be. The consequences of each value to be tested is significant. What might the end results be of each value to be tested? This is a highly significant question to answer on the part of experimentalists. Thus, there are consequences for each value tested within a larger geographical context. Values that have failed can be analysed and evaluated. A new synthesis might then be in the offing. Values are developed and tested to improve the human situation, or move from the present to what should be. The 'what should be' is openended and does not consist of closed, dogmatic ideals.

Morris and Pai wrote:

But what, to ask the final question, ought we to want? To this the experimentalist has no answer, for it is an ultimate question and ultimate questions have no answers. Since values are to be found in the context of experience, we will have to find out what we ought to want in this selfsame, relativistic circumstances of ordinary experiencing. There simply is no absolute answer.

The only kind of sensible answer one can give is that people ought to want what they in fact do want when presented with all the alternatives and the knowledge of their consequences—which is no more than saying that a community of human beings employing a kind of public sharing of preferences and values and being intelligent about the whole business, can come to a working notion of the kind of civilization they would like to build, that is to say, the values that they would like to work for and attain. But in the working for and attaining of these values, other values have a tendency to suggest themselves. Humanity's valuing becomes, then, a constant creation of and accommodation to the changing moral environment about it. As the consequences that flow from humanity's principles change, the principles themselves change.

## B. Aesthetics and Experimentalism

What is beautiful in the experiences of individuals in society? Why is selected music, art, drama, architecture, poetry, and other forms of literature relevant in comparison to other works involving aesthetics? There are no absolute standards in making judgements involving the aesthetic world, according to experimentalists. Each creative product and endeavour is tested in society. Individuals in society then accept, reject, or are neutral toward the endeavours of artists in diverse fields. Works of art then are tested in society. Artists notice the consequences of their products and processes. What is prized highly in a given place and time might not receive those ratings in other contextual situations, past and present.

Gelger writes the following involving change in society:

Nor can liberal education be simply content with efforts to preserve the past; it must take the lead in understanding, criticising and directing cultural change. That knowledge of the past contributes mightily to an understanding of the present is indubitable, and the present interpretation takes full account of it. But that the past be cultivated for its own sake is something else again. It is present culture, nor past, which is our problem. This does not signify that the more conservative view of liberal education is unconcerned with present-day problems. But it would appear that the spector of discontinuity haunts the traditionalist here as elsewhere. Apparently he would prepare the adolescent by steeping him in historical materials of classic dimensions, and in the grand style, and then turn him loose, as an adult, on modern problems.

## Realism in Education

Realists tend to believe that an objective real world exists, independent of any observer. The objective world can be known as it truly is. Opinions and subjective judgements of persons is not important. Rather, through objective methods, the real world can be known through experimentation. Knowledge is held as being tentative until empirical evidence indicates hypotheses needs changing. Rigid controls are necessary in scientific experiments in order that end results are truly objective. A learner needs ample experiences in science and mathematics since these curriculum areas emphasise objectivity and are highly relevant. Individuals live in a world of science. Each must respect natural law to live fully. Thus, principles of science in the curriculum should reflect the desire of learners to abide by the laws of nature. The laws are empirically based and not subject to the personal values and ideals of individuals. Content in science can be desired in mathematical terms. Mathematics contains exact and precise subject matter independent of the feelings and beliefs possessed by any one individual.

In addition to science and mathematics being significant in the curriculum, other academic areas also contain objective content. Numerous students have been made of words that learners need to master in reading. The identified words, gathered from carefully controlled studies indicate those that have high utilitarian values and, if mastered, will cut down tremendously on reading errors among leaners. Similar scientific studies have been made pertaining to words that pupils needs to master in spelling. The identified words are useful for mastery learning. They consist of a core of words which all should learn to spell to minimise spelling errors on the part of learners. Other curriculum areas which contain objective subject matter for pupil mastery include history (containing precise content on names, dates, places, and events) as well as geography. The latter has emphasised objective geographical phenomenon in time and place. The phenomenon include a study of rivers, valleys, plains, plateaus, oceans, mountains, and sees, among others. Wahlquist wrote:

Realists generally agree in stressing the need of making philosophy scientific. A major part of the realistic programme of reform consists in emphasising the close relation of philosophy to the sciences. There are those who think that the proper procedure for philosophy is to utilise the method of abstraction perfected in mathematics and made the basis of all scientific investigation. Generally, realists are agreed that the method of scientific analysis is the fundamental approach. The ultimate department of the truth of an idea is regarded as something beyond mere personal satisfaction, something external to the personality, and not dependent upon it. Consequently, truth must be discovered by objective means, as free as possible from the subjectivity of the experimenter. The realist is interested in the temperature of the room as registered by a gadget, not the impressions of the persons in the room.

## A. Values, Ethics, and Realism

Realists believe that values change. The change, however, is much more gradual, as compared to the thinking of experimentalists. Scientific methods need to be utilised by persons, individually and collectively, to ascertain that which has value. Opinions adhered to by individuals are subjective in content. Agreed upon adopted values need to be independent of person feelings of involved human being. Thus, objectivity is a key concept to emphasise in valuing according to realism as a philosophy of education. Human beings can discover and attain objective values.

Nature contains laws revealing what is right or wrong. Individuals can discover these laws of nature. To be successful in life, individuals must abide by the laws of nature. Morris and Pai write the following pertaining to natural law:

> We may now speak of a nature-borne law of conduct that controls us quite as insistently and absolutely as does natural and ultimate truth. Natural law in ethical theory is usually called "moral law," and by this term we mean a law of right and wrong, that is embedded in the very structure of nature. Nature contains not just laws of gravity, thermodynamics, energy, and metabolism—that is, laws of the behaviour of completely material, subhuman entities; it contains laws of human behaviour as well.
>
> In speaking of group behaviour, we can cite economic and political laws, like the oft-cited Law of Supply and Demand or Lord Acton's famous law of political life: "Power corrupts; absolute power corrupts absolutely." Likewise in individual behaviour, says the Realist, there is a moral law intrinsic to the real, natural world that we must obey if we choose to be human beings. Injunctions against taking human life, lying and cheating are the kinds of moral taboos that may go unwritten,

even unspoken, in human societies; but they are nevertheless constantly operative in our lives, for they persist in time-space and exert their force on the conduct of all people in as immanent a way as the law of gravity. Furthermore, everyone knows these laws, whether we can utter them or not. We live "within" them, if not always "by" them.

Morris and Pai further wrote:

Now, pure theory in epistemology is the analogue of natural or moral law in ethical discourse. Moral law is that law of behaviour which is beyond human utility, which is unconnected with our human interests or desires, and which consists merely in a statement of what the universe requires in the say of conduct. Moralists search for these laws for the same reason scholars search for truth: just to know them. These laws have no immediate application, but because they are laws of the cosmos we desire to know and hold them for their own sake. If they are seen to apply to this or that circumstance, so much the better; we make use of them. But the first and primary business of ethics is to know and commit oneself to natural and moral value.

Realists then believe there are moral laws independent of the observer's feelings and values. These laws must be discovered and observed. Objectivity and the methods of science are key concepts to emphasise in realism philosophy.

## B. Aesthetics and Realism

What is beautiful? Nature has answers to this question. The answers are objective and do not involve human subjectivity. Personal biases should be omitted. The real environment contains beauty in nature. A beautiful bed of roses can be known as they truly are, independent of the observer. The roses do not need modifying and revising to emphasise beauty. They are beautiful in and of themselves.

Compositions in music also possess inherent beauty. Beauty in music is there, independent of observers and can be discovered. Observers therefore agree in time and space, as to what exemplifies beauty in music.

Feats in architecture need to adhere to natural law for a structure to remain endurable. Beauty inherently can reside within these structures. Independently of the observer, architectural endeavours either endure or do not endure. Nature has much to say in terms of which structures adhere to the laws of nature.

Wahlquist wrote:

The realist is impressed with the objectivity of the external world. He holds that knowing is a process of disclosure, not one of creation of the "reals." The real world is not subject to human whim and caprice. Experience is always experience-of, experience plus, reality. Furthermore, reality sets the limits upon experience in both form and content.

The external cosmos is beyond the powers of man to know; the most he can hope for is to learn some of its secrets and to harness its forces. What he learns constitutes the great body of science, the only factual knowledge extant. One thing is sure; the world can go on without the aid of man; in some respects he is a fool to pass judgement upon it. In fact, if he would learn anything about the world, he must go about it objectivily, eliminating selfish desires and personal preferences. The more he learns about this external world, in which he has his beginning and the forces of which constitute and control his being, the safer his future will become.

In short, the realist tries to keep himself and his preferences out of the picture. In this respect, he feels that he clashes with both the idealist and the pragmatist. He desires to see things "realistically," or as they actually are.

## Existentialism in Education

Existentialists believe that one exists and then purposes need to be found or developed. The individual self then determines his/her own goals in life. There are no absolutes or exact guidelines in life to choose what is right or good. Each person must select and make decisions. To avoid making decisions is to lack being human. The choice then is to go along with the crowd. However, to be human involves making decisions.

The only broad criterion for existentialists to follow in choosing is to make moral decisions in a complete atmosphere of freedom. Others should definitely not decide one's destiny. One did not ask to be born and yet each person must make authentic decisions.

Moral decisions are difficult to make. An environment of awe exists in making authentic choices.

Which objectives, learning activities, and evaluation procedures should be inherent in an existentialist curriculum? Existentialists believe in each person choosing objectives. In the school setting, the goals may be selected by learners with teacher guidance within the framework of an open-ended curriculum. A highly structured curriculum in which the teacher selects each objective for pupil attainment is definitely frowned upon by existentialists. Much teacher-pupil planning should, of course, be in the curriculum. Learners need to learn to choose and to make decisions, according to existentialists.

The teacher needs to emphasise ends, means, and evaluation procedures which stress the importance of pupils becoming increasingly responsible for personal freedom. The teacher should definitely not be a policeman. Rather, teachers realise their roles as providing for a open environment in order that the learner may select sequential experiences.

The teacher needs to encourage learners to study morality and moral standards in life. Each pupil must be encouraged to stand up for relevant purposes in life. The involved pupil needs to accept the philosophy that no person receive values, inherently, to accept. Rather, each choose his/her own destiny and values in the curriculum of life. Purposes in learning need to come from the learner, and not from the teacher or others in society.

Learners should realise that significant decisions must be made in life which involve "fear and trembling." The everyday routine decisions made by any one person generally are not moral choices. Choices made which reflect ultimate changes in society in moving toward standards of morality are indeed relevant and goal-oriented.

Pupils need to realise that important knowledge is subjective and not objective or science-oriented. Each decision made in life involves personal decisions in reaching a goal or goals. Thus, subjectivity in subject matter content is important. Literature, history, poetry, art, music, drama and architecture are indeed significant curriculum areas. Each person can assist in shaping society in a moral direction when the humanities and the arts become an inherent part of the personal individual to make significant decision.

Each person makes or breaks himself or herself. No other person or being is responsible for personal choices and decisions made. Each individual then must assume responsibility for consequences of decisions made. Blaming others for what happened in life is meaningless, according to existentialists. Each pupil needs to learn to accept responsibilities for thoughts, deeds, and action. Bowyer wrote the following involving the thinking of Soren Kierkegaard (1813-1855), an existentialist:

According to Kierkegaard, truth is not some prefebricated absolute that can be found outside the individual. Truth, he believed, can be attained only by an existing individual, for truth is subjectivity. A description of man's existential situation involves a distinction between man's present state—the way he is—and his potential state—the way he ought to be. There is a moment in the life of the individual from what he is essentially to his existential condition, from essence to existence.

Bowyer further writes:

Kierkegaard's existentialism emphasises individualism (not the group or crowd) subjectivity (not science or empirical means of arriving at truth), introspection (looking within the personal self, and feeling (rather than objective facts). Kierkegaard emphasised freedom of the individual rather than logic, mechanism or determinism.

Existentialism then emphasises:

1. Individual rather than group endeavour. The individual exists and then chooses his/her own destiny.

2. **Subjective ideas rather than the methods of science in making choices and decisions. The individual is the decision-maker.**
3. **Feelings rather than subject matter which can be tested and proven. The arts then need heavy emphasis in the curriculum. Individuals possess feelings. Decision-making is an awesome responsibility.**
4. **Each individual makes the self rather than living a predetermined life. The person chooses, makes choices, and decides. There is no predetermined life in which individuals merely do what was preordained prior to the lifespan of anyone person.**

## A. Values, Ethics and Existentialism

The existentialist looks to the self for values. The major criterion to use in the valuing domain is morality. Moral decisions are to be made in a completely free environment. Other beings must not dictate what is ethical or right. If the self looks toward others for ethical decisions, one no longer is human.

Existentialists believe that each person to be human, needs to select that which is ethical. Permitting others to choose for the personal self evades responsible behaviour. Each must choose what to do ethically within a contextual situation. Consequences for making choices rests with the chooser. Strumpf writes the following pertaining to the thinking of Jean Paul Sartre, a leading existentialist:

Man is always obliged to act in a situation, that is, in relation to other person, and consequently his actions cannot, must not, be capricious, since he must take responsibility for all his actions. Moreover, to say that man must make his essence, invent his values, does not mean that one cannot judge human actions. It is still possible to say that one's action was based either upon error or upon self-deception, for any man who hides behind the excuse of his passions, or by espousing some doctrine of determinism deceives himself. To invent values, says Sartre, means only that there is no meaning or sense in life prior to acts of will. Life cannot be anything until it is lived, but each individual must make sense of it. The value of life is nothing else but the sense each person fashions into it.

The inner directed person making moral decisions and accepting the consequences is important to existentialists. The existentialist does not blame other for outcomes of decisions made since the self made the choice. Choices made may not lead in the direction of making friends. In fact, alienation may occur as a result of speaking out and doing in the morality domain. The existentialist may well be linked to one acting alone and by himself or herself.

What then is ethical to do? The individual must make this decision to be human. No one else can make this choice for the chooser. Self-gratification or focusing upon personal gains does not agree with criterion set forth by existentialists. Rather, what is moral needs emphasis in the decision-making area.

### B. Aesthetics and Existentialism

What represents beauty in the natural and social environment? The individual, alone, is responsible in choosing what is beautiful. Responsibilities in making the choices lie with the chooser, alone. Choices made may lead to unhappiness and feelings of loneliness. In making choices, the personal decisions are made in relationship to other human beings, never in a vacuum. Beauty is in the eyes of the beholder. Universal standards cannot apply. Each person is unique and experiences life in its everyday tragedies, anxieties, and tensions. Art products need to reflect situations in life experienced by the individual.

## Idealism and the Curriculum

Idealists believe in an idea centred curriculum. One cannot know the real world as it truly is, but the observer obtains ideas only pertaining to natural and social phenomenon. Universal ideas rather than specifics are significant, according to idealism, as a philosophy of education. The universal ideas remain rather stable in time and place, and are not subject to continue change.

Idealists believe that people individually and collectively are finite beings. Each individual is limited as to what can be achieved or attained. However, each person must move away from being finite to become increasingly like the infinite.

In moving away from finiteness and in the direction of infiniteness, the person must experience an idea centred curriculum. Mind is real and mind then must be developed. Horne writes the following pertaining to mind being real.

Mind Is real. (a) Education, as a human process with a meaning to spell concerning the truth, seizes upon mind as the final useful appendage to the organism in its upward evolution. That which nature by spontaneous variation, the struggle for existence, and the survival of the fit bestows as its last best gift to the organism, education seizes upon to improve, this raising evolution from the unconscious natural to the conscious mental plane. The highest type of selective agency of man,— education, lays hold upon the highest selected product of nature, —mind, for further improvement, thereby indicating mind as the highest type of temporal reality. Education by its emphases practices the saying of Sir William Hamilton, viz., "In the world there is nothing great but man; in man there is nothing great but mind." The school and also the other more general educative agencies of civilization lay all their stress upon mind as the most valuable, the most useful, the most real element in life. Chosen last as the result of an incalculably long, prehistoric process of natural selection, mind is become first. Education may be pardoned its ontological boldness if it questions reflectively whether the reality it selects as ultimate is not the ultimate reality. Is not reality mental?

There are selected curriculum areas which idealists believe are relevant in guiding pupils in the direction of the infinite mind. Universal ideals need to be acquired by learners in an idea-scentred curriculum. Providing needed subject matter include the academic areas of:

1. reading, literature, history, and geography;
2. writing including grammar, spelling, punctuation, capitalisation, among other skills, needed to present clearly communicated ideas;

3. mathematics and science;
4. other curriculum areas, such as health, art, music, and physical education.

Academic areas which assist in developing the mind are superior to other curriculum areas. However, to develop universal ideas, a learner needs to be perceived historically—intellectually, morally, emotionally, socially and physically. Human beings need to move beyond the observable to truly understand natural and social phenomena. Theodore. Greene writes the following:

My first presupposition, or basic assumption is that man finds himself in a complex environment which he can in some measure know and to which he can more or less successfully adapt himself. This assumption falls halfway between radical skepticism, on the one hand, and all forms of absolutism or authoritarianism on the other. I believe that man can know something, but not everything; that he can know many things with increasing clarity and assurance, but that he can never, because he is incorrigibly finite, know anything with complete certainty and finality.

## A. Values, Ethics and Idealism

The idealist educator emphasises universal values and ethics be developed by learners. Universal criteria are enduring in time and place. Secular and sacred literature in diverse historical periods of time as well as in numerous geographical regions have emphasised a universal ethic in the Golden Rule. "Do unto others as you would have them do to you" represents a universal standard of conduct.

Idealists advocate that experience of the senses is superficial compared to depth searching in terms of what is valuable. To understand and use the Golden Rule is complex. Understanding the universal ethic and how it operates in diverse situations is not easy. It is even more difficult to develop needed skills in utilising the Golden Rule in every day experiences in life. Theodore. Greene writes the following involving liberalism in ethics pertaining to idealism, as a philosophy of education:

Liberalism, so conceived, has its own basic values which it must defend at all costs because they condition its vitality and, indeed, its very existence. The specific virtues which it must espouse and the vices which it must combat can usefully be defined in the context of a liberal educational policy. The three basic liberal virtues are: (a) serious concern; (b) intellectual and moral integrity; and (c) profound humility; the three corresponding vices are frivolous or cynical indifference, lack of integrity, and arrogance. Teachers should be hired only if they possess these three virtues, in addition to intellectual competence, and they should be fired either for incompetence or for exemplifying any one or more of these three vices. It should also be the prime concern of the school assiduously to foster these virtues and combat these vices in its students as well as to cultivate whatever intellectual and creative talents they may possess.

## B. Aesthetics and Idealism

What makes for beauty in art, music, architecture, and literature, among other creative endeavours of human beings? Human beings are limited or finite. The finite needs to continually move in the direction of the infinite. What exists in the natural and social environment needs improving in moving away from the limited to the unlimited. The creative artist then attempts to present universal content in artistic endeavours. Products in art reveal beauty in terms of ideals stressed. Ideas pertaining to the natural/social environment need to express artistically that which is enduring and universal going beyond what the sense portray is significant. Human beings need to search for beauty. Troy Organ writes the following:

Values are intrinsic to the world. The world supports and sustains men as they attempt to increases the values in the universe. The intuitive insights of the artist and the prophet give more accurate glimpses of the real nature of the world than do the hypotheses and the experiments of scientists. Since the view of the world as spiritual is held by those who believe the world to be ideal-like but do not believe in God, as well as by the supernaturalists, the term "idealism" is used to identify this position, even though the word is extremely ambiguous. Among its many uses it denotes both those who believe the world is mind-dependent, that is, reality is always and necessarily the object of a perceiving mind (subjective idealism) and those who believe the world is spiritual rather than physical and does not depend upon being perceived (objective idealism).

## In Summary

Philosophy of education has much to say in terms of implementing objectives, learning activities, and evaluation procedures in the curriculum.

The experimentalist educator believes that learners need to identify and solve relevant problems in a changing society.

Realists advocate using methods of science to obtain precise information involving the real world as it truly is.

Existentialists emphasise the importance of the individual making subjective moral commitments within an irrational world.

Idealists believe that universal standards and generalisations need discovering in moving from the finite to the infinite being.

Educators need to be students of philosophy. Diverse philosophical strands provide guidance in developing the curriculum.

# Content in the Curriculum

A frequent question that arises pertains to *what* should be taught in terms of content in the curriculum. This is a problem that pertains to scope and sequence. Johann Frederich Herbart (1776-1841) felt that literature and history were the most important curriculum areas in the schools. These curriculum areas might then aid students in developing good moral character. Jean Jacques Rousseau (1712-1778) believed that science (the natural environment) should provide major learnings for pupils. Johann Hienrich Pestalozzi (1746-1827) felt that actual objects and the real environment should be the major source of learnings for pupils.

## Certainty of Content to be Learned

There are selected educators who are fairly certain pertaining to content that should be learned by pupils. The Essentialists under the leadership of William Chandler Bagley (1874-1946) believed that learnings could be identified which all pupils were to develop. The three Rs. (reading, writing, arithmetic) history, English, as well as discipline and obedience, may then provide basic content for all learners. Thus, a core of content exists which pupils need to learn and master.

Advocates of behaviourally stated objectives feel that content generally can be identified which pupils are to master. Behaviourally stated objectives generally are written prior to teaching a given set of learners. These objectives are written with much precision. Thus, after instruction, it can be observed and measured if these kinds of objectives have been achieved. Notice the following measurable objectives:

1. The pupil will list in writing the names of all continents on the planet earth.
2. The pupil will write a fifty-word paragraph on how climate affects agricultural crops grown.
3. The pupil will read a one hundred-word essay on global peace and state two facts and two opinions contained in the writing.

Behaviourally stated objectives can be written on the *recall* of information level or on complex levels of thinking. Each of the above objectives indicates that after teaching a given set of learners, it can be measured if the objectives have or have not been achieved. Prior to teaching then, the teacher generally selects what learners are to learn. Thus, certainty exists in the mind of the teacher as to *what* pupils are to learn. The teacher then selects content which pupils are to master.

## Humanistic Objectives in Education

Humanistic education emphasises the development of the attitudinal dimension of individuals. Thus, pupils must have a chance to engage in decision making as to *what* is to be learned as well as the media to use in learning. To be sure, the teacher should have adequate opportunities to structure the learning environment in a flexible direction. However, within that structure, pupils have opportunities to determine objectives and learning activities. They also have opportunities to assess their own achievement.

According to humanists, learners need to be assisted in developing well socially and emotionally in that concern for others is an important objective to achieve. Thus, the affective, attitudinal, or feeling, dimension becomes important in developing. Developing the self concept of the learner becomes vital. The learner basically selects tasks that are of interest and can be completed successfully. Joy in learning must be in evidence. The learning activities are selected on what appears to be relevant to the learner. Interest, relevancy, and success in learning are viewed from the child's unique perception. Thus, in selecting content to be learned in humanistic approaches to learning, the child is a major determiner when decisions are made. There is considerable less certainty as to which content pupils are to learn when stressing humanistic education as compared to the use of behaviourally stated objectives.

## Content and Programmed Learning

In programmed learning, the programmer decides upon what pupils are to learn. The sequence or order of these learnings is also determined by the programmer. Thus, once the learner is ready for utilising selected programmed materials, he/she might participate in the following sequentially:

1. Read selected content and view the related picture or pictures.
2. Respond to an item, such as a completion item.
3. Check the personal given response against that provided by the programmer.
4. Correct answers given by students may be its own reward and provides for reinforcement.
5. If responses given were incorrect, the learner now knows the correct answer, and is also ready for the next sequential programmed item.

The above named steps may be followed again and again in programmed learning. In determining content to be learned, the programmer in developing programmed materials determines what pupils are to plan and in what order. There seems to be considerable certainty in terms of what pupils are to learn as perceived by the programmer.

## Content and the Structure of Knowledge

Selected educators strongly emphasise that pupils inductively develop structural ideas as identified by academicians. For example, social scientists from colleges and universities may identify major generalisations from their academic areas of speciality. Thus, key structural ideas are identified by historians, geographers, political scientists, sociologists, anthropologists, and economists. Learners in the school curriculum may realise these ideas inductively on their own understanding level. Pupils should understand these ideas on a more complex level, continuously, as they progress through their respective years of schooling. Learners might also use the methods of acquiring and assessing information as emphasised by these academic specialists in the social sciences. Thus, if pupils worked as historians, an ample number of primary sources among other learning experiences, might be utilised in gathering data. Or, pupils working as geographers, should utilise as well as make maps and globes, among other sources, in gathering and recording data.

The structure of knowledge approach in providing content for learning emphasises degrees of certainty as to content which pupils are to learn. College and university professors then need to identify and agree upon as to what the structure of knowledge is in each of the identified disciplines of content.

## Problem Solving in the Curriculum

All individuals face major as well as minor problems in life. Problems in society can be identified. Questions arise when considering and observing the natural and social environment. From these problems and questions, related information may be gathered in terms of solutions. Hypotheses or answers are then obtained in relation to the problem or question. Ultimately the hypotheses are accepted, modified, or refuted. These steps would generally represent a framework for describing problem solving situations in learning. John Dewey (1859-1952) was a leading advocate in emphasising problem-solving situations in the curriculum. Problem solving indicates the need for information from any and all academic disciplines and curriculum areas as long as it is relevant in realising solutions. Thus, subject matter is used in solving problems. Disciplines or academic areas used in solving problems have their importance as they aid in working toward solutions. Knowledge then is selected on the basis of being instrumental in solving problems. Thus, content is important in terms of problem solving activities in the school setting as well as the curriculum of life. Content cannot be selected in terms of what will be relevan[illegible] or to identification of relevant problem areas. Once problem areas have been identified, subject matter becomes important in terms of realising desired solutions.

**Content and the Learner**

It is important for pupils to develop relevant understandings, skills, and attitudes. The question arises as to what is relevant for pupils to learn. There certainly are disagreements in thinking when educators attempt to answer this question. It is important to be able to solve personal problems as well as problems that exist in society. Only they can individuals improve their lot as productive members in society. Content used in problem-solving is relevant to the problem being pursued. Thus, in problem solving activities, it cannot be determined with certainty as to *what* content is relevant for all learners in the school setting or in life.

Learners' interests vary from individual to individual. It appears that ample opportunities should be given to learners in making decisions pertaining to *what* to learn. Since learning styles differ from pupil to pupil, it would be sound to have learners engage in decision-making as to how desired learnings are to be achieved.

Academicians on the college and university level can make tremendous contributions in terms of identifying content pupils are to learn. Their recommendations might also pertain to pupils utilising methods of gaining knowledge that specialists in the diverse disciplines use. Pupils might select tasks in learning where these structural ideas are developed inductively using procedures recommended by academicians.

Learners have diverse learning styles. It may be of benefit to selected learners to utilise programmed materials in achieving relevant understandings, skills and attitude objectives.

**In Summary**

The history of education states which curriculum areas or skills were perceived to be of utmost importance in learning as determined by selected famous educators. Certain educators emphasised which discipline or curriculum area was most important for learners. Herbart, for example, felt that literature and history were the most relevant curriculum areas for learners.

More recent approaches in determining relevant content for learners pertain to the following:

1. The teacher, as well as principals or supervisors, determining prior to teaching what pupils are to learn.
2. Pupils deciding what to learn as well as the media of learning within a flexible framework largely determined by the teacher.
3. Programmers determining what pupils are to learn and in which sequence these learning are to be obtained.
4. Academicians identifying key structural idea for pupils to achieve utilising methods of procedure recommended by specialists in the diverse disciplines.
5. Pupils with teacher guidance identifying relevant problems or questions from a stimulating environment, thus working in the direction of obtaining possible solutions.

# Scope in the Curriculum

What should learners study in the curriculum? What students are to acquire involves the concept of scope? There are diverse means of determining scope in teaching and learning.

## Problem Solving

Problem solving experiences might well provide the majority of learnings for students in ongoing units of study. The teacher, first of all needs to set the stage to stimulate learners to identify problems. Reading and nonreading materials may be used. The teacher then needs to encourage problem identification by learners. Once the problems have been identified, learners with teacher guidance may choose reference sources (concrete, semi-concrete, and abstract experiences) to gather data directly related to chosen problem areas. Students may then offer a hypothesis (or hypotheses) in answer to the problem. The hypothesis needs testing in action, and modifications made, if needed. The steps in problem solving are flexible, not rigid nor formal.

Thus, problem-solving activities emphasised exclusively in any unit of study emphasised the scope of that unit. Students with teacher leadership can select and solve meaningful problems in the curriculum. Each learner may perceive selected problems as being relevant and be actively involved in their solution, whereas other problematic situations are sensed as being irrelevant and thus avoided. There, of course, are opportunities for learners to select and work on that which is relevant. Interest in what is deemed relevant provides effort in learning. Learners presently need to choose and solve problems as present active citizen in society.

**Essentials in the Curriculum**

There are educators who believe that essential learning exist which *all* learners need to attain without exception. These basic learnings are necessary in order to be successful as an adult in society. Education then becomes significant in terms of *preparing* the learner for life in society. What is basic or essential for students to learn?

Most educators advocate pupils being able to add, subtract, multiply, and divide within the framework of counting and whole number systems, as a minimum. To be able to read effectively, many teachers and supervisors emphasising the basics believe that students should master phonics skills, syllabication, and context clues needed to identify unknown words in reading in diverse curriculum areas. Minimal comprehension skills in reading also need mastering, such as reading to follow directions, to acquire facts, to gain main ideas, and to understand sequential content.

In the writings curriculum, essentialist educators advocate pupils understanding grammar and usage. Writing needs to follow conventional standards. All frills and fads in the curriculum need to be avoided. Only, essential learnings need emphasising. Correct spelling of words is essential and possesses objectivity in terms of content.

In social studies, no doubt, history and geography have stood the test of time and should be emphasised strongly. History and geography contain relatively objective content. Other social science disciplines of economics, political science, anthropology, and sociology are of lesser importance. The latter are newer social science disciplines and might not possess the objectivity of history and geography. Nor have these disciplines stood the test of time in the school curriculum.

William Chandler Bagley (1874-1946) author of the *Essentialist Manifesto* wrote:

Because new configurations are unpredictable, however, it does not follow that there are no permanent, or at least relatively permanent, elements of culture. It is true that the world of today is a different world from the world of 1913 and from the world of 1929; it is even different today from what it was yesterday; but this does not mean that everything has changed. Two and two still make four; the square on the hypotenuse is still the sum of the squares on the two other sides of the right-angle triangle; light and radiation still vibrate through interstellar space at a rate between 186,000 and 186,300 miles a second; the winds that blow still follow the laws of storms; Huckleberry Finn and Treasure Island still delight youth; and the Sistine Madonna is just as beautiful as of yore.

From the point of view of social welfare and progress, too, there are some virtues that have not lost their value. Frugality and thrift may not be so significant as they once were, but respect for life, respect for law, consideration for the feelings of others, and plain, everyday honesty are still important. Even though fewer believe in a literal hell, there are other means of holding passions within leash. Even in the past many men and women who rejected religious dogmas lived honest, considerate, decent and respectable lives.

Bagley believed that enduring, permanent subject matter can be identified which *all* learners need to attain. These are essential learnings, basic to all students in the curriculum.

What should be the *scope* of the curriculum in the thinking of essentialists? Those learnings that are basic for all pupils to attain. Unnecessary subject matter needs to be weeded out. Subject matter (vital facts, concepts, and generalisations) as well as relevant skills (reading, writing, and arithmetic, in particular) need to be taught well in each significant academic area (history, geography, and science included).

Provision needs to be made for individual differences in teaching and learning. However, no curriculum area can be taught emphasising the interests of learners only. The will of the pupil also needs to be involved in ongoing activities. Thus, the learner must reach out and attain basic ideas and abilities. This represents the scope of the essentialists curricula.

## The Structure of Knowledge

Jerome Bruner from Harvard University advocated pupils achieving structural ideas, as perceived by academicians in their respective academic areas of specialty. Thus, for example, linguists have identified nine patterns of sentences which recur again and again in the English language. All written and spoken sentences may be classified into one of these patterns of sentences. Also, linguists have identified four means of expanding (enlarging) sentences to clarify oral and written communication. The concept of stress, pitch, and juncture also are important in the communication arena, according to linguists.

Social scientists (historians, geographers, political scientists, economists, sociologists, and anthropologists) each in their subject matter specialties have attempted to identify key concept and generalisations worthy of pupil attainment. The same is true of scientists (biologists, chemists, botanists, zoologists, astronomers, physicists, and geologists) who also have attempted to select structural content for learners to acquire. Bruner wrote:

the curriculum of a subject should be determined by the most fundamental understanding that can be achieved of the underlying principles that give structure to that subject...Organising facts in terms of principles and ideas from which they may be inferred is the only known way of reducing the quick rate of loss of human memory.

Jerome Bruner emphasised that pupils learn through inductive strategies. Thus, pupils may learn via discovery methods by finding out on their own. What might be learned inductively? Structural ideas identified by academicians in their academic areas of speciality. Methods of inquiry utilised by these subject matter specialists should also be used by pupils on their own unique levels of achievement.

What is the scope of the curriculum, according to Bruner? Structural ideas identified by academicians in each curriculum are a studied by pupils. Which processes to be acquired by learners should be included in scope? Inductive procedures and methods used by academicians to attain structural content.

Three kinds of materials are to be utilised sequentially by learners within the framework of methodology. Enactive (manipulative materials), iconic (audio-visual materials to guide pupils to achieve mental images), and symbolic materials (listening, speaking, reading and writing).

Jerome Bruner later called for a deemphasis upon structure of knowledge approach in the curriculum:

If I had my choice now, in terms of a curriculum project for the seventies, it would be to find the means whereby we could bring society back to its sense of values and priorities in life. I believe I would be quite satisfied to declare, if not a moratorium, the something of a de-emphasis on matters that have to do with the structure of history, the structure of physics, the nature of mathematical consistency, and deal with curriculum rather in the context of the problems that face us. We might better concern ourselves with how these problems can be solved, not just by practical action, but by putting knowledge, wherever we find it and in whatever form we find it, to work in these massive tasks. We might put vocation and intention back into process of education, much more firmly than we had it there before.

A decade later, we realise that process of education was the beginning of a revolution, and one cannot yet know how far it will go. Reform of the curriculum is not enough. Reform of the school is probably not enough. The issue is one of man's capacity for creating a culture, society, and technology that not only feed him but keep him caring and belonging.

## Measurable Objectives in the Curriculum

Behaviourists emphasising specific objectives implementation in teaching-learning situations believe that teachers need to determine what pupils are to learn. The total number of sequential objectives for learner attainment represents *scope* of the curriculum. In ascending order of complexity, learners may, as a result of experiencing learning opportunities, attain each measurable end. After instruction the teacher may measure if a learner has/has not attained a precise end. If an objective has not been attained, a revised or new teaching strategy may need to be provided to guide learner success in goal attainment.

Within each curriculum area, committees of teachers in each grade level may identified vital, measurable ends for pupils to achieve. Perhaps, a reasonable number in each curriculum area must be achieved by any one pupil in order to be promoted to the next grade level at the end of a school year. Talented and gifted students, of course need to achieve as many measurable objectives in each curriculum area within each school year, as is feasible. Each learner needs to achieve optimally.

Instructional Management Systems (IMS) advocate that teachers and supervisors develop measurable objectives in each curriculum area for an entire school year, prior to their implementation. No doubt, an entire school year may be needed to accept, edit, and write worthwhile specific ends for pupils to achieve.

Again, the total number of measurable objectives for pupils to achieve in any school year represents the *scope* of the curriculum. Or, the total number of objectives for students to achieve within the allotted years of school to attend also represents the concept of scope in the curriculum.

## In Conclusion

Which criteria should be emphasised in determining the scope of the curriculum?

1. breadth of content, skills, and attitudes need to be adequately broad to include vital learnings for pupils.
2. subject matter, abilities, and affective ends need to possess perceived clarity to learners, as well as to teachers and supervisors. Vague, meaningless learnings need to be omitted or modified. Quality general objectives or measurably stated ends may both adhere to the criterion of clarity of ends.

3. learners need to perceive interest, meaning, and purpose in attaining vital learnings within the framework of scope in the curriculum.
4. sequence or order of learnings to be acquired by learners need to be derived from accepted scope in the curriculum. Thus, identified scope needs to be transferable to determine sequential objectives for pupils achievement as the latter progress through diverse lessons, units, and years of schooling.

After scope has been determined in the curriculum, adequate consideration needs to be given to sequence in learning opportunities for students.

Orlich, et. al. wrote:

By sequencing instructional tasks, one assumes that a student can better master any organised body of knowledge or discipline when the content is carefully interrelated. One also assumes the learning of skills or knowledge in a systematic manner helps the student to develop those skills that ultimately aid with information-processing, that is, thinking. Finally, one assumes that the closer that sequenced instruction approaches a "programmed format", the greater the probability for student success.

If we are willing to accept these key assumptions about schooling, then sequencing has two basic purposes. One is to isolate knowledge (a fact, concept, generalisation, or principle) so that the student can understand the unique characteristics of the selected information or to isolate a thinking process so that the student can master the process under varying conditions. The second purpose is to relate the knowledge or process being taught to the larger organised body of knowledge. The first function-isolating what is being taught helps *make learning more manageable*, and the second function—relating the information—*makes learning more meaningful.*

## REFERENCES

Bagley, William C. *Education and Emergent Man*. (New York: The Ronald Press Co., 1934), pp. 151-152.

Bruner, Jerome S. *The Process of Education*. Cambridge, Mass.: Harvard University Press, 1960, pp. 31-32.

Bruner, Jerome S. "The Process of Education Reconsidered," in Robert R. Leper, ed., *Dare to Care / Dare to Act*. (Washington, D.C.: Association for Supervision and Curriculum Development, National Education Association, 1971), pp. 29-30.

Orlich, Donald C. et. al., Teaching Strategies. *A Guide to Better Instruction*. Lexington, Mass., 1985, Page 54.

# Philosophy and Goals in the Curriculum

Each learner and supervisor possesses a philosophy of curriculum development. It might even be that the educator in the school setting can not verbally state the perceived philosophy. However, there are a set of beliefs which provide guidance in performing selected acts and deeds, in teaching lessons and units. How then does a specific philosophy provide direction in determining educational goals?

## Essentialism in the Curriculum

Essentialists believe there are essential learnings that *all* pupils need to achieve. Thus, a common body of basic knowledge and skills exist which a learner must acquire to become a successful adult in society. The pupil then needs to be prepared to fulfill life's responsibilities at a later time. Education is a preparation for life.

Which learnings are essential for pupils? The three r's (reading, writing and arithmetic) generally are considered basic for all. Thus, to ultimately contribute effectively in society, the learner presently needs to become a proficient reader, and writer, as well as compute effectively in addition, subtraction, multiplication, and division. Goals can be developed to reflect worthwhile learnings for pupils pertaining to the three r's. The goals may be stated as general or measurably stated ends.

Are there additional essential curriculum areas for pupils to master relevant knowledge and skills? The older social science disciplines of history, political science, and geography are generally included. No doubt, anthropology, sociology, and economics would be minimised. The curriculum area of science also has solid subject matter for each learner to acquire.

Essentialists believe that frills and fads should be eliminated in the curriculum. Thus, even physical education may be placed on the back burner in terms of a relevant essentialists curriculum. Which objectives might then be emphasised by essentialists?

1. Skills in word recognition in reading, such as use of phonetic analysis, structural analysis, context clues, picture clues, syllabication, and configuration clues.
2. Skills in comprehension in reading, such as reading to scan, skim, acquire facts and main ideas, as well as reading to obtain sequential ideas. Higher cognitive comprehension skills involve critical reading, creative reading, and reading to solve problems.
3. Skills in utilising the table of contents, the index, the glossary, dictionary, almanac, atlas, the card catalogue, encyclopaedia, and other vital reference sources.
4. Skills to spell words correctly, write legibly, develop coherent sequential paragraphs, punctuate sentences correctly, and capitalise words properly.
5. Possess adequate knowledge to present subject matter content in depth in the writing curriculum.
6. Skills to correctly add, subtract, multiply, and divide when utilising counting numbers, whole numbers, rational numbers, and integers. Definite high standards need to exist in arithmetic, algebra, geometry, calculus, probability, and statistics for all learner to achieve.
7. Knowledge pertaining to key structural ideas in history, political science and geography.

8. Solid subject matter in the science curriculum. Thus, pupils need to achieve vital subject matter in astronomy, geology, chemistry, physics, biology, zoology and botany. Methods of acquiring subject matter for pupils should resemble those utilised by scientists in a laboratory setting.

Peter F. Oliva writes the following pertaining to essentialism:

The goals of the essentialist are primarily cognitive and intellectual. Organised courses are the vehicle for transmitting the culture, and emphasis is placed on mental discipline. The 3 r's and the "hard" (i.e. academic) subjects form the core of the essentialist curriculum. In one sense the essentialist tailors the child to the curriculum whereas the progressivist tailors the curriculum to the child.

Oliva also states:

The aim of education, according to essentialist tenets, is the transmission of the cultural heritage. Unlike the reconstructionalists who would actively change society, the essentialist seeks to preserve it. Again, unlike the reconstructionalists who would seek to adjust society to its populace, the essentialists seek to adjust men and women to society.

**Perennialism in the Curriculum**

Perennialists believe in having learners acquire Great Ideas of the past. These ideas have stood the test of time (history) and space (the planet earth). Ideas expressed by recent writers may be culled as time goes on, and thus not become an inherent part of enduring subject matter. The Great Books is an important concept in curriculum development, according to the thinking of perennialists. Perhaps, one cannot come up with better literature, than that expressed in the Great Books. The thinking of Buddha, Confuscious, Plato, Aristotle, John Locke, John Stuart Mill, and Bertrand Russell, among others, cannot be improved upon. The Great ideas of these thinkers continually remain to be significant. Brubacher writes the following pertaining to Robert M. Hutchins, late leading advocate of perennialism:

> Education, rightly understood, Hutchins claimed, was a cultivation of the intellect, which, he further claimed, was the peculiar excellence of all men of all times and in all places. The intellect was to be cultivated through studies of permanent worth. These were to be found in the great books of all time. A "great book" was one that is contemporary with my age. But in order to read great books the student must know how to read them. To learn this he must go back to a curriculum made up of the trivium of grammar, logic, and rhetoric together with some formal mathematics from the quadrivium.
>
> Exacting as were Hutchin's standards, he did not limit liberal education to the few, as had the genteel tradition. On the contrary, the liberal education he had in mind was for the whole student population in so far as they had time to pursue it.

Which objectives might then be emphasised by perennialists?

1. skills in reading so that abstract learnings might be acquired by learners;
2. knowledge of significant ideas written by classical writers whose thoughts are enduring;
3. skills in logical thinking, including deductive reasoning developed by Aristotle;
4. skills in writing in order to develop outlines, summaries, precise, critiques, and originality in compositions;
5. attain essential subject matter in general education, such as in literature, science, history and geography.

**Existentialism in the Curriculum**

Existentialists believe that individuals should choose their own goals and their own personal destinies. There are no absolutes nor infinite guidelines to follow. Each person then makes or breaks himself. First, one exists, then the self needs to find purpose or reasons for living. This is an awesome responsibility. There are so many choices to be made. Complete freedom must be in evidence for any being to make the decisions.

The concept of morality is important to follow when any decision is made. Thus, moral decisions need to be made in an unrestrained environment. How any choice made affects others must be considered in the moral dimension. The chooser must accept complete responsibility for decisions made. Others can not be blamed for the consequences of an act or deed. The end result of doing may be positive. It can also result in alienation. Decisions made may offer dread, fear, and anxiety to the chooser.

Existentialists do not like the following concepts for adherence purposes: authoritarian, group or committee endeavours (unless the latter is personally chosen), universal ideas (unless the decision maker selects these ideals without compulsion), objective content, and externally imposed obedience. What is within the person needs to come to the surface in making choices. The locus of control is from within rather than from without.

Ozman and Craver write the following pertaining to Jean-Paul Sartre's thinking on existentialism:

In his philosophical works, Sartre views the human predicament in terms of the lonely individual in an absurd world. Essentially, he views human existence as primarily meaningless, for man is thrown into the world totally without meaning, and any meaning which man encounters in the world he must construct himself. The development of meaning is an individual matter, and since both the world and individual man are without meaning, man has no justification for existing... Thus, when man steps back and views himself as he really is, he sees that nothing determines him to do anything, for all the absolutes, rules, and restrictions are simply the puny and absurd creations of man. If there are no primal restrictions, then there is no determinism. Everything is possible. Man is absolutely free, or as Sartre puts it in his own characteristic terminology, "man is condemned to be free."

Which curriculum areas might existentialists then emphasise?

1. subjective academic areas such as art, music, literature, and history. The human condition is best represented in these curriculum areas.
2. units of study in learning more about the self and others. Pupils should realise feelings, beliefs, and concerns possessed by individuals.
3. emphasis upon decision-making representing subjective, not objective content. Learners need to make decisions which they will personally feel accountable for.
4. moral acts and deeds need to be emphasised in the curriculum of life.

## Realism in the Curriculum

Realists believe that one can know the natural and social environment as it truly is. One's values, attitudes, and beliefs are then omitted in terms of learning about objective phenomena. Using the methods of science to acquire subject matter allows learners to achieve that which is factual and real. Subjectivity is then minimised and perhaps omitted. In utilising the methods of science the learner must:

1. Observe carefully and identify factual statements.
2. Use the senses of sight, hearing, taste, touch, and smell to acquire information. Feelings and opinions must be minimised in teaching-learning situations.
3. Realise that content in science is subject to testing, modifying, and verifying.
4. Use a variety of reference sources to acquire objective subject matter.
5. Communicate results accurately and objectively.
6. Develop skills to predict consequences in testing a hypothesis (or hypotheses).
7. Develop attitudes involving a desire to utilise methods of science to gain subject matter.

8. Use mathematics to express science content in a precise, quantifiable manner.

The supervisor or teacher adhering to realism, as a philosophy of education, has selected recommendation to make in the curriculum. First of all, pupils need to experience comprehensive science courses of study. Thus pupils need to achieve vital objectives in astronomy, biology, botany, zoology, chemistry, physics and geology. Objectives in each of these academic areas should be stated in measurable terms. After instruction, the teacher may measure if each pupil has/has not attained desired ends. Alternative teaching strategies need to be utilised for those pupils who have not achieved stated objectives.

Secondly, the teacher needs to provide a variety of learning activities to guide learners to attain desired ends. Thus, excursions, films, filmstrips, slides, educational television, transparences, illustrations, encyclopaedias, basal science textbooks, and other reference materials might be utilised by pupils to gather needed information.

Thirdly, learners with teacher guidance need to use laboratory methods of acquiring subject matter. Subject matter attained should be utilised to solve problems and test hypotheses. Learners then need to have ample opportunities to work as scientists do, within a laboratory setting.

Fourthly, learners need to have a quality current events curriculum involving the world of science. In each academic discipline in science, current happenings occur at an accelerating rate.

Wahlquist writes the following pertaining to realism, as a philosophy of education:

Realists generally agree in stressing the need of making philosophy scientific. A major part of the realist programme of reform consists in emphasising the close relation of philosophy to the sciences. There are those who think that the proper procedure for philosophy is to utilise the method of abstraction perfected in mathematics and made the basis of all scientific investigation. Generally, realists agreed that the method of scientific analysis is the fundamental approach. The ultimate determinant of the truth of an idea is regarded as something external to the personality, and not dependent upon it. Consequently, truth must be discovered by objective means, as free as possible from the subjectivity of the experimenter. The realist is interested in the temperature of the room as registered by a gadget, not the impressions of the persons in the room.

## Idealism in the Curriculum

Idealists believe in an idea-centred curriculum. The person cannot know the real world as it truly is or exists. However, ideas can be acquired dealing with natural and social phenomena.

A quality general education curriculum may provide needed ideas to learners. Thus, pupils need to study literature, history, geography, grammar, writing, mathematics, and the sciences to secure needed subject matter. Pupils may then achieve universal ideas. Universal ideas, or generalisations are supported by facts. The board generalisations, however, are more important than factual content. A well educated person then achieves universal content which has stood the test of time and space. This person becomes less finite and moves increasingly in the direction of the Infinite.

Ethically, an idealist attempts to practice the universal standard of 'do unto others as you would have others do unto you'. Or, as Immanuel Kant (1724-1804) believed-others need to be treated as ends and not as stepping stones or means to an end (the Categorical Imperative).

The human mind develops order and sequence of perceptions noticed in the environment. Ideas, not object per se, are significant. The human mind needs developing through a variety of rich experiences. Only then, might subject matter guide learners to lean in the direction of the Infinite being.

Morris and Pai wrote the following:

In idealism, therefore, we need to provide reality into two major divisions: the apparent and the real. The "apparent" realm is our day-to-day experience as mortals. This is the region of change, of coming and going, of being born, growing, aging and dying; it is the realm of imperfection, irregularity, and disorder; finally, it is the world of trouble and suffering, evil and sin. The "real" world, fortunately, is not like this. It is the home of the mind, the realm of ideas, it is the home of eternal qualities, of permanence, of regularity, or order, of absolute truth and value.

Of the two, quite obviously, the ideal is of higher rank. Not only is it distinct from the world we know directly, but it stands existentially higher. This is because perfections reign there. Perfect things are those things that do not change; they don't have to. What conceivably could they change to? Since eternal ideas do not change, they represent a perfect order.

Which objectives might an educator stress with idealism as a philosophy of education?

1. a thorough understanding of vital subject matter. Academic areas to be understood by learners include literature, history, geography, mathematics, science, writing and grammar. Each pupil also needs to attain skills necessary to acquire and use information, such as achieve abilities to read, write, and compute effectively.
2. gaining generalisations and main ideas (universals in subject matter) in the curriculum.
3. an attitude of wanting to increase the fund of subject matter acquired. Each person needs to become less finite and move in the direction of becoming an Infinite being.
4. a mental set in desiring an idea centred curriculum.
5. a will to learn. Interest in learning is not adequate. Each person must possess a will or desire to learn. This is true even if obstacles exist in the learning environment.

**Experimentalism in the Curriculum**

Experimentalists believe that ultimate reality is what one experiences. Human beings cannot know the real world as it truly is and exists. But the person has experiences in the natural and social environment. Humans experience change, not a stable environment. Scenes and situations change continuously. Since change abounds, problems arise. These problems need identification. Related content needs to be acquired from diverse reference source in order to secure information pertaining to the identified problem. A hypothesis, needs testing in an actual life situation. The end result may be to accept, modify, or refute the hypothesis.

Life itself consists of identifying and solving problems. The school curriculum should not be separated from what is relevant in society. William James states the following pertaining to pragmatism, also known as experimentalism.

Pragmatism represents a perfectly familiar attitude in philosophy, the empiricist attitude, but it represents to me, both in a more radical and in a less objectionable form than it has ever yet assumed. A pragmatist turns his back resolutely and once in for all upon a lot of inveterate habits dear to professional philosophers. He turns away from abstraction and inefficiency, from verbal solutions, from bad *a priori* reasons, from fixed principles, closed systems, and pretended absolutes and origins. He turns toward concreteness and adequacy, towards facts, towards action, and towards power. That means the empiricist temper regnant and the rationalist temper sincerely given up. It means the open air and possibilities of nature, as against dogma, artificiality, and the presence of final truth.

Which objectives in general, do experimentalist educators advocate in the curriculum?

1. *The methods of science*. Content needs to be objective and as unbiased as possible to be of use in the real world.
2. *Problem solving procedures*. Learners with teacher guidance need to identify and solve relevant problems.
3. *Experience a miniature society*. What is relevant in society needs to be emphasised in the school

curriculum. School and society are integrated, not segregated entities.

4. *Subject matter used to solve problems*. Preferably, subject matter should not be learned for intrinsic values, but rather to resolve problematic situations.

## In Conclusion

Teachers and supervisors need to study, appraise, and ultimately implement vital strands from diverse philosophical schools of thought. In teaching and learning, each student needs to (a) perceive purpose (b) experience interest (c) attach meaning.

## REFERENCES

1. Brubacher, John S. *A History of the Problem of Education*. Second Edition. New York: McGraw Hill Book Company, 1966.
2. Ediger, Marlow, *Relevancy in the Elementary Curriculum*. Kirksville Missouri, Simpson Publishing Company, 1975.
3. James, William, "What Pragmatism Means" As Quoted in *Selected Readings in the Philosophy of Education*. (Joe Park, Editor), New York: The Macmillan Company, 1968.
4. Morris, Van Cleve, and Young, Pai. *Philosophy and the American School*. Second Edition. Boston: Houghton-Mifflin Company, 1976.
5. 'Oliva,' Peter F., *Developing the Curriculum*. Boston: Little, Brown and Company, 1982.
6. Ozman, Howard and Carver, Sam, *Philosophical Foundations of Education*, Columbus, Ohio, Charles E. Merrill Publishing Company, 1976.
7. Wahlquist, John T. *The Philosophy of American Education*. New York: The Ronald Press Company, 1942.

# Issues in the Curriculum

There are selected issues needing identification, study and analysis. Teachers and supervisors must be cognizant of vital dilemma situations and be able to justify the position taken, within an issue, in emphasising a specific philosophy in teaching-learning situations. Which issues might be relevant to identify?

1. measurably stated versus general objectives.
2. the basics versus an activity centred curriculum.
3. prescribed courses for all students as compared to numerous elective classes.
4. general education for all as compared to a project method in providing for individual differences.
5. teachers sequencing objectives for students as compared to learners ordering learning experiences.
6. a subject centred versus an experience centred curriculum.
7. teacher appraisal of student progress contrasted with self-evaluation by learners of their individual achievement.
8. large group instruction as compared to individualised teaching for students.
9. separate subject versus a correlated, fused curriculum.
10. behaviourism as compared to humanism as psychologies of learning in the curriculum.

Whichever philosophy of teaching and learning is selected, each learner needs to attain optimally.

## Theories in Curriculum Development

Each teacher and supervisor needs to possess vital concepts and generalisations in developing each curriculum area. Theories provide a generalised set of assumptions which provide direction in selecting objectives, learning activities, and appraisal procedures.

## Humanism in the Curriculum

A humanist educator places much emphasis upon the following concepts:

1. trust among learners;
2. freedom to explore and learn;
3. creative behaviour;
4. openess in curriculum;
5. self-realisationl;
6. decision-making;
7. empathy;
8. curiosity and uniqueness;
9. love and belonging;
10. esteem;
11. security.

Humanist oppose teachers choosing objectives, learning activities, and appraisal procedures for learners. Rather, the learner must be involved in determining ends and means to pursue in ongoing units of study. To involve pupils in planning the curriculum, trust among participants must be inherent. Only then, according to humanists, might pupils achieve optimally or develop self-realisation. The self concept of the learner is of utmost importance. Learners need to have ample opportunity to achieve esteem or worth for understandings, skills, and attitudes possessed. Thus, creative behaviour rather than rigid formal teacher determined ends need emphasis in the curriculum. Each learner needs to be accepted as having intrinsic worth.

Combs, et. al. wrote the following involving perceptual psychology (humanism) in guiding self-realisation within human being:

Perceptual psychology provides us with an essentially hopeful view of persons. For several generations we have lived with a conception of persons as almost exclusively the products of the forces exerted upon them, prisoners of the past. In such a view the responsibility of human beings lies always outside themselves and human potentiality lies largely at the mercy of forces over which an individual has little or no control. If human behaviour is exclusively the product of stimuli, then no one can ever be held responsible for his behaviour and the solution to our great human problems must be placed in the hands of some great mind who knows where the people should go and a cadre of assistants skilled in manipulation to make sure they get there.

The perceptual view of persons is far more hopeful. It sees the dynamics of behaviour as inside a person and each human being, therefore, in far greater measure the architect of his own existence. If behaviour is the product of perception, the limits of human potentiality are restricted only by the richness, extent, and availability of perceptions in a person's personal field of meaning. The eventual possibilities for human beings in such a view of human potentials are beyond comprehension. Motivated by a basic need for self-actualisation we can also be assured the expression of such potential will be in positive directions if we can find the means to set free.

Questions which might be raised pertaining to humanism involve the following:

1. Are learners adequately responsible to truly choose tasks which are challenging and worthwhile?
2. Will the essentials (basics) such as reading, writing, and arithmetic receive adequate attention in the curriculum?

3. **How can teachers and supervisors determine if pupils are progressing satisfactorily, without the use of measurable ends?**

## Behaviourism and the Curriculum

Behaviourist stress the following concepts in structuring the curriculum:

1. programmed learning;
2. reinforcement;
3. sequential steps in learning;
4. observable and measurable responses;
5. precise objectives;
6. stimulus response;
7. conditioning;
8. primary and secondary reinforcers;
9. tokens;
10. practice, drill, and tutorial instruction.

Behaviourists oppose using teacher-pupil planning procedures in the curriculum. Rather, the programmer selects objectives, learning activities, and evaluation techniques. Programmers generally field test their materials in pilot studies to eliminate situations in which pupils make numerous mistakes in responding to sequential items. A programmer may need to add small sequential steps at specific points to minimise errors made by learners. Thus, for example, programmers can develop programmed materials in which pupils read a short selection, respond to a completion item, and check their own personal answer with that provided by the programmer. If a learner was correct in the response made, he/she is rewarded and reinforcement is in evidence. If an incorrect response was made, the student still knows the correct answer, as given by the programmer, and is also ready to tackle the next sequential item. The procedures of read, respond, and check might be utilised again and again in programmed materials. Each sequential step of learning is observable and measurable.

Primary reinforcers may be provided learners for being successful in learning. Primary reinforcers may involve providing pupils with prizes and inexpensive badges for goal attainment. Secondary reinforcers might involve utilising tokens which learners may exchange for prizes at appropriate intervals. Woolfolk, et. al., wrote the following involving the concept of reinforcement:

Whether the consequences of any action are seen as positive or negative depends on the individual's perception of the event and the meaning it holds for her or him. The chance to give an oral report to the entire class may be a very desirable event for one student and a task to be avoided at all costs for another. In order to determine whether an event is positive or negative, we must watch the person involved and see whether the person will work to attain it or work to avoid it. If the person will work to attain the event it is considered reinforcement for that person.

Returning to the ABC notion of behaviour, we can say that behaviours that are followed by reinforcement (positive consequences) are likely to be repeated in the future. When you see the term reinforcement you should immediately think about a behaviour increasing. Put another way, whenever you see a behaviour persisting or increasing over time you can assume that something is reinforcing that behaviour. It is important to remember that the event reinforcing the behaviour may not seem that positive to you. Reinforcement is defined by its effect of increasing behaviour. Students who are sent to the principal's office repeatedly for the same offense may be indicating that the trip is in some way reinforcing for them even if such a trip hardly seems reinforcing to you.

A related version of behaviourism is for the teacher to write measurably stated objectives. Next, the teacher chooses learning activities for pupils to attain desired ends. After which, the teacher measures which learner has/has not attained an objective. The objective must be achieved before a learner moves on to the next sequential objective. A different teaching strategy may need to be utilised by a pupil who was not successful in goal achievement.

Good and Brophy wrote the following involving the utilisation of behaviourally stated objectives:

Mager (1962) and others have stressed the importance of behavioural objectives for instructional planning. Intelligent planning begins with the identification of clear and sensible objectives. Before you can plan systematically, you must know what you want to accomplish. Clear-cut objectives provide both a starting point for planning and a rationale for evaluating the effectiveness of instruction.

Mager and others, who stress the term "behavioural objectives," believe that expected outcomes should be expressed in language that stresses what the student will be expected to do. Specific descriptions should be provided that make it easy to observe whether or not the objectives have been met. We believe that this approach is valuable, but we prefer the broader terms "learning objectives" or "objectives."

These terms broaden the consideration of objectives to include purely cognitive objectives (the student will understand the concept of "area"), in addition to purely behavioural ones (the student will be able to compute the areas of geometric figures correctly). The term "behaviourally objective" is more precise, but it is also more restricted in meaning and is associated with explicitly behaviouristic theories and procedures. These and other aspects of the behavioural objectives movement have led to its rejection by many who are not sympathetic to behaviouristic approaches.

Partly for this reason, and partly because it is more general and applies just as easily to purely cognitive objectives, we will use the term "learning objectives".

Questions which might be raised pertaining to the use of behaviourism in the curriculum involve the following:

1. Can worthwhile objectives be identified, rather continuously, which might be stated in observable and measurable terms? Might vital attitudinal goals be stated measurably?
2. Should stated objectives reflect input from learners in curriculum development?

3. Who should be involved in sequencing objectives, the programmer, the teacher, or pupils with teacher guidance?

## Structure of Knowledge and Inductive Learning

Selected educators advocate that teachers emphasise and pupils acquire structural ideas in each academic area. The structure of knowledge is generally identified by academicians on the college/university level in their respected areas of speciality. Thus, for example, linguists cooperatively have identified sentence patterns in the English language such as:

1. the subject-predicated pattern;
2. the subject-predicate-direct object pattern;
3. the subject-linking verb-predicate adjective pattern;
4. the subject-linking verb-predicate noun pattern;
5. the subject-predicate-indirect object-direct object pattern.

Any sentence in the English language, basically, can be placed into a sentence pattern. The patterns may well be preceived to emphasise a structure of knowledge in spoken and written English. Each of the sentence patterns may be expanded using one or more of the following means:

1. using modifiers (adjectives and adverbs);
2. using appositives;
3. using compounding (compound nouns, verbs, adjectives, adverbs, as well in independent clauses to develop compound sentences);
4. using subordination (dependent adjective, adverb, and noun clauses).

Pherix wrote the following involving structural content in the curriculum:

My thesis, briefly, is that all curriculum content should be drawn from the disciplines, or, to put it another way, that only knowledge contained in the disciplines is appropriate to the curriculum.

Exposition of this position requires first that we consider what is meant by a "discipline". The word "discipline" is derived from the Latin word discipulu, which means a disciple, that is, originally, one who receives instructions from another. Discipulus in turn stems from the verb discere, to learn. Etymologically, then, a discipline may be construed as knowledge the special property of which is its appropriateness for teaching and its availability for learning. A discipline is knowledge organised for instruction.

Basic to my theme is this affirmation: the distinguishing mark of any discipline is that the knowledge which comprises it is instructive—that it is peculiarly suited for teaching and learning. Implicit in this assertion is the recognition that there are kinds of knowledge which are not found within a discipline. Such nondisciplined knowledge is unsuitable for teaching and learning. It is not instructive. Given this understanding of what a discipline is, it follows at once that all teaching should be disciplined, that it is undesirable to have any instruction in matters which fall beyond the disciplines. This means that psychological needs, social problems, and any of a variety of patterns of materials based on other than discipline content are not appropriate to the determination of what is taught-though obviously such nondisciplined considerations are essential to decision about the distribution of discipline knowledge within the curriculum as a whole.

Each academic discipline contains structural ideas or key generalisations for learners to attain. Advocates of the structure of knowledge philosophy believe that learners need to acquire learnings inductively. Academicians in their respective areas of speciality generally obtain knowledge in an inductive manner. To emphasise induction, the learner may identify a problem. Next, data from a variety of reference sources needs to be obtained, directly related to the problematic area. Thus, a hypothesis can be achieved. The hypothesis then needs testing in a variety of ways, after which it may be modified, if necessary. Learners in the curriculum should utilise similar/same methods of inquiry as do academicians in their personal professional bodies of knowledge.

Structural ideas should be acquired as a result of learner inquiry utilising the flexible steps of problem solving.

Questions which may be raised involving the structure of knowledge philosophy of teaching and learning include:

1. Can pupil interest be developed to achieve adult determined subject matter content? Or, should learners acquire subject matter learnings which meet their own personal needs and interests?
2. Are learners adequately mature and skilled to utilise methods of gaining subject matter knowledge deemed useful by academicians?
3. Who should determine that which learners are to achieve? Academicians? Teachers? Programmers? Pupils?

## In Closing

Three models were presented in curriculum development:

1. Humanism with its emphasis on pupils selecting what to learn within a flexible framework.
2. Behaviourism with its stress upon measuring each step of learner progress.
3. Structure of knowledge methods with its emphasis upon key generalisations to achieve by learners. The structural ideas have been chosen by academicians.

Teachers and supervisors need to select objectives, learning activities, and evaluation procedures which aid each pupil to achieve optimally in the curriculum.

## REFERENCES

1. Combs, Arthur W. et. al. *Perceptual Psychology, A Humanistic Approach to the Study of Persons*. New York: Harper and Row, 1976.
2. Ediger, Marlow, *Relevancy in the Curriculum*, Kirksville, Missouri: Simpson Publishing Company, 1975.
3. Good, Thomas L. and Brophy, Jere, *Educational Psychology*. New York: Holt, Rinehart, and Winston, 1977.
4. Morris, Van Cleve, and Young Pai, *Philosophy and the American School*; Second Edition, Boston: Houghton Mifflin Company, 1976.

5. Pherix, Phillip H. "The Uses of the Disciplines as Curriculum Content." *The Educational Forum*, March, 1962.

6. Popham, James, *Knowledge of Results*, (Filmstrip and Cassette), Vincet Associates, 1969.

7. Ragan, William B., and Shepherd, Gene, *Modern Elementary Curriculum,* Sixth Edition, New York: Holt, Rinehart, and Winston, 1982.

8. Tyler, Ralph, *Basic Principles of Curriculum and Instruction*, The University of Chicago Press, 1950.

9. Woolfolk, Anita E. et. al. *Educational Psychology*. Englewood Cliffs, New Jersey: Prentice-Hall, Inc., 1980.

# Designing the Curriculum

Curriculum design is an important factor when guiding optimal learner progress. How the curriculum is designed will make considerable differences in terms of the kinds and types of objectives to be emphasised, which learning opportunities to implement, as well as how pupils will be evaluated. The focal point of teaching and learning is the pupil. Thus school administrators, teachers, and other workers in the educational setting must continually have the pupil in mind when making modifications and changes in the curriculum.

## Objectives of Instruction

Objectives for learner attainment may be stated as general and/or specific. The trend presently is to write behaviourally stated objectives. Thus the objectives of instruction are written precisely and in measurable terms. A pupil either does or does not achieve any one objective as a result of teaching and learning. The objectives leave little leeway in interpretation as to their meaning or meanings.

Quantifiable results are available from pupils after tests have been given. A pupil's results may be shown as a per cent of correct responses, a percentile rank, a quartile deviation, or in standardise units such as standard deviation from the mean.

A student teacher (ST) supervised by the writer in the public schools believed strongly in the use of general objectives within the framework of unit teaching. The ST emphasised that not all salient goals can be stated in measurably, particularly the attitudinal ends of instruction. Her thinking was that attitudinal are the most important objectives of instruction. Thus if good attitudes are in evidence, knowledge and skills goals have a better chance of being achieved as compared to a learner having negative affect. After the lengthy discussion, the ST said she definitely did not agree with vague objectives such as to develop a democratic citizen or to make good readers of pupils. She mentioned that general objectives can be clearly stated and be open-ended to leave leeway for some diversity of outcomes. The ST gave the following examples of clearly stated general objectives which she favoured above those of being behaviourally stated:

1. to develop within the learner an understanding of how animals with backbones are classified;
2. to develop within the pupils skill to read critically;
3. to develop within the learner an understanding of problems existing between Palestinian Arabs and Jews of Israel over the hand formerly called Palestine.

None of the above objectives have an indicator, nor are they stated in a manner which permits measuring to ascertain learner progress. However, each objective is clear as to what will be taught and learned. For example, in objective number one above, pupils will learn to classify vertebrates in terms of being fish, amphibians, reptiles, birds, or mammals.

The ST believed that too many teachers and educators have hangups on the need to state objectives measurably. She stressed that these kinds of objectives are very time consuming in their writing. Sometimes an entire class session of fifty minutes in a methods of teaching class was spent in determining how to write three affective objectives so that they are stated in measurable terms. The question then arises if attitudinal or affective ends could be written as general objectives. Consider the following general objectives stressing attitudes:

1. to develop within the pupil a desire to read more library books pertaining to the unit presently being taught. Certainly in general, the teacher can notice

if the learner is reading an increased number of library books. More time, no doubt, should be spent on planning for instruction than what so often is spent on determining precise, behaviourally stated objectives;

2. to develop within the pupil feelings of respect toward others. Again, in general, one can notice the kinds of behaviour learners reveal towards each other;

3. to develop within the pupil an attitude of wanting to work harmoniously with others in committee setting. The teacher here may notice which pupils work well in achieving, growing, and learning as compared to pupils who waste time and/or disrupt what others are doing.

The writer believes, in time, debate will open up pertaining to the advantages of using general objectives as compared to behaviourally stated objectives in the curriculum.

A further debate involved here is which kinds of objectives should receive most emphasis. Thus when comparing knowledge, skills, and attitudinal ends, which one or ones should be stressed most in teaching-learning situations? Relevant facts, concepts, and generalisations are salient to learn. But so are skills of critical and creative thinking as well as problem solving of tremendous importance. Perhaps, it is ridiculous to attempt to separate knowledge from skills objectives due to skills of critical and creative thinking as well as problem solving being inherent or a definite part of acquiring subject matter. Being successful learners, attitudes become a by-product of instruction. Also attitudes that are positive assist pupils in wanting to learn and achieve.

**Sequence of Objectives**

In designing the curriculum, someone must establish sequence for the learner. The classroom teacher might well determine this sequence or order of pupil's attaining objectives. The teacher then logically selects which order the objectives should be arranged so that each pupil may learn as much as possible. Thus the teacher will arrange the objectives in ascending order of complexity. A logical curricula is then in evidence. The behaviourally stated objectives movement would harmonise well with the logically devised curriculum.

Toward the other end of the continuum, the curriculum might stress teacher-pupil planning. Here, in context, pupils and the teacher or team of teachers plan cooperatively what the former are to learn. Pupil are then increasingly empowered to select from among alternatives what (the objectives) to learn. A skillful teacher is needed who has good rapport with learners and can work harmoniously with each pupil. The teacher is very knowledgeable about subject matter, skills, and attitudes that learners need to attain. He/she enjoys working with young people and guides their optimal progress. The teacher here is a facilitator, helper, and guide, not a lecturer or dispenser of information. Since pupils are heavily involved in curriculum development, a psychological curriculum is in evidence. The individual pupil then develops a sequence in learning. Sequence resides within the pupil, not teachers, textbooks, nor other reference materials. General objectives would harmonise well with a psychological curriculum. General objectives permit diversity of outcomes as a result of teaching-learning situations.

### Learning Activities

Who should select learning activities for pupil goal attainment? Toward one end of the curriculum, the teacher is basically in charge of choosing activities and experiences. The teacher must then select those learning activities which are meaningful, purposeful, and provide for individual differences. These opportunities must guide pupils to attain the objectives of the unit or course of study. If behaviourally stated objectives are stressed in teaching-learning situations, the learning opportunities must align with the objectives of instruction. Thus the activities and experiences guide pupils to achieve the behaviourally stated objectives, largely or only.

Toward the other end of the curriculum, the teacher may stress a learning centres philosophy of instruction. An adequate number of centres needs to be in evidence with approximately five tasks written on small cards for each centre. A pupil may omit tasks not perceived to be worthwhile. Time on task is vital, but enough tasks are available so that each pupil may work on sequential tasks that possess perceived purpose. The writer has had ST's who believed that a learning centres philosophy may work effectively only if pupils possess self discipline and have an inward desire to learn. The ST's further stressed that learners not possessing these traits need more structure in the curriculum in which the teacher selects the objectives, learning opportunities, and appraisal procedures. Perhaps, what is being said here is that individual differences determine how the curriculum will be organised.

**Arrangement of Subject of Subject Matter**

Pupils may acquire subject matter by emphasising a single academic discipline in teaching-learning situations. For example, in an ongoing unit of study, the teacher may teach history only. Historical content would then provide the scope and sequence of the unit being taught. It would be extremely difficult to stress only one academic discipline such as history in teaching-learning situations; however, in a single subjects approach in organising subject matter to be taught, history here would receive predominate emphasis.

At the turn of this century, numerous educators advocated that subject matter needed to be taught as being related and not as separate subjects. Thus for example, history and geography could be taught as related in an ongoing unit of study. These two disciplines relate well. When learners are gaining knowledge about a historical event, the event is also located on a map and globe which then brings in geography in the curriculum. Presently, many history teachers believe in the correlated curriculum which relates, in this case, history and geography.

Over the years, ST's supervised by the writer have advocated more integration of content. Thus, these students believe that political science, economics, sociology, and anthropology should be stressed also in ongoing units of study. A few ST's have expressed caution with bringing in too many academic disciplines within a unit to be taught. The concern here is that a survey procedure of teaching will then be in evidence. Thus, there could be too much ground covered in a very short period of time resulting in a loss of depth teaching strategies.

**Evaluation Procedures**

There are many procedures available to evaluate pupil achievement. Teacher observation is a very common approach. The teacher here must keep up with salient trends in the curriculum to use standards of excellence to appraise learner progress. A very recent trend in evaluating pupils' achievement is to use the portfolio philosophy. In a portfolio, there should be representative products of a learner's achievement. Thus written work, tape recordings of reports given in class, art products, test results, snapshots of objects constructed, among other items, may be a part of the part folio. Careful assessment of the portfolio is needed to thoroughly appraise each pupil's attainment.

In addition to teacher observation and the use of portfolio's, the following separate methods may be used:

1. teacher written test items such as true-false, multiple choice, essay, matching, and short answer or completion tests;
2. criterion referenced and norm referenced tests;
3. checklist and rating scales;
4. discussion quality.

**In Summary**

The design of the curriculum needs careful consideration so that each pupil may attain as optimally as possible. Learners must experience interest, meaning, and purpose in teaching-learning situations. Quality design in the curriculum may well guide pupils individually to attain as much as possible.

# Organising the Curriculum

Writers in education extoll the virtues of the integrated curriculum. Thus, different academic areas may be taught as being related to each other. There are a plethora of advantages here, in that one idea may trigger another when learners in school perceive the relationship of knowledge. However, this may make for surface learning rather than indepth teaching in many cases. My beliefs are that both depth teaching and surface learning may need to be stressed in the curriculum. Time does not exist during the school day where all learnings are taught in depth when the integrated curriculum is being emphasised. Thus, choices will need to be made as to what should be taught in depth and what should stress surface learning. Then too, there are objectives which are more worthwhile for student achievement than others. These will require indepth teaching even when a curriculum purports to be integrated, such as in unit teaching. Within the framework of indepth teaching, students should and generally do indicate they perceive relationship of knowledge. Thus, both the integrated and separate subjects curriculum have merit in teaching. This chapter will attempt to indicate the separate subjects curriculum to also have considerable merit, within or outside the unit teaching concept.

## When Should the Separate Curriculum be Emphasised?

There are times on the elementary and middle school levels when a unit on a separate subject should be stressed. Even then, it is difficult to emphasise a single curriculum area. Why?

Reading, writing, listening and speaking (oracy) will be inherent since these four language arts areas cut across all curriculum areas taught. This is true on the secondary and higher education levels in particular. For example, there is hardly a university course which does not require much reading, many written papers and note taking discussions, and careful listening to lectures. Beyond that, academic areas seemingly cannot survive unless there is integration of content, such as in history, e.g. historical events occur, not only in time, but also in space or regions as in geographical areas. However, a separate subject such as geography may need to be taught indepth such as in a massive tsunami/earthquake occurrence. Devastating natural disasters may well then need to be taught in depth.

As supervisors of student teachers, we have observed student and cooperating teachers teach entire units on Maps and Globes which indicated a strict geography emphasis except for the usual four language arts areas of listening, speaking, reading, and writing being inherent. The maps and Globes separate subjects unit gave the student teacher and cooperating teacher ample opportunities to teach indepth north/south and east/west reference lines, flora and fauna in different regions, cause of seasons, and the rotation of the earth on its axis as well as its revolving around the sun, among other geographical concepts. This may be done with sacrifices made toward other related factors such as time in history. But, the separate subjects versus the integrated methods of curriculum design does involve a trade off. There are definite criteria to use when cmphasising a separate subjects curriculum within a unit of study or as a emphasising unit of study:

1. the concepts and generalisations need to be vital to understanding specific phenomena. Thus, more time needs to be spent with the use of a variety of activities to achieve the objective(s);
2. these understandings cannot be taught effectively in an integrated curriculum;
3. it is necessary to teach a separate subjects unit indepth and relate the concepts and generalisations later to an integrated unit of study;

4. a current events happening involving a major disaster (tsunamis and earthquakes) may need to be taught as a separate unit due to its recency and importance;
5. a watered down curriculum results when too much integration of content is an end result. There is no time then to focus upon certain necessary learning.

## An Integrated Curriculum

Integration of subject matter has definite values for student learning and retention. It almost appears as if subject matter is truly related, but is separated into component parts as students progress throughout the different years of schooling. The separation of content into specific areas occurs increasing so on the secondary and higher education levels. For example, history classes alone may be divided into a component of medieval history. Within a course on medieval history, the professor may focus upon the guilds which, for example, had three levels of achievement such as the apprentice, the journey man, and the master. Perhaps, this is perceived as being important from the point of view of marketing quality products and receiving a fair wage for its day. Or, three levels of training in approaching knighthood such as entering as a page, then being promoted to a squire, and finally being dubbed a knight.

The integrated approach in curriculum development tends to emphasise problem solving as learning opportunities. Thus, within an ongoing unit of study, students identify a problem. The problem presents a dilemma, and is of interest to students in the school setting. Time and deliberation is inherent in problem solving. Each problem needs to be clearly identified so that there are possibilities of concise solutions. Vague, identified problems may be too broad to be solved. After students with teacher guidance are satisfied with the problem's clarity, the necessary reference sources need to be chosen. These consist of materials necessary in problem solving. Thus, concrete (objects, items, museums, human resources, field trips, and realia), semi-concrete (illustrations, pictures, study prints, internet, world-wide web, video tapes, CDs, DVDs, among others), as well as abstract (print sources, discussions, reports, cassettes, and tapes) may be used to secure needed information for the problem(s). After thorough investigation of reference sources, an hypothesis, as a tentative solution to the problem, should be developed. The hypothesis, being tentative, is subject to rejection, modification, or change.

Problem solving stresses the use of higher levels of cognition with analysis (separating face from opinion, the accurate from inaccurate, as well as fantasy from reality). Creative thinking is also emphasised in problem solving. Here, novelty, uniqueness, and originality are involved in perusing the diverse reference materials. It is different from other learning opportunities in that:

1. memorisation of subject matter is not stressed, but knowledge is acquired and used to solve relevant, identified problems;
2. subject matter is not divided into component parts, but used holistically in dilemma situations;
3. the use of subject matter from any academic discipline is emphasised in forming an hypotheses or solution;
4. utilitarian purposes or practicality is inherent in finding solutions to problematic situations;
5. life like situations require that applications may be made of what has been learned.

## In-between Positions

There are teachers who prefer in-between positions involving the separate subjects versus the problem solving or integrated curriculum. One point on a line segment, representing this dichotomy, involves a correlated curriculum. Correlation involves teachers relating two academic disciplines such as economics and geography. When students, for example, achieve objectives pertaining to the kinds of agricultural crops grown in a specific region, geography as an academic discipline is involved. Temperature readings, amount of rainfall, and types of soil are involved in producing different kinds of farm crops.

When the monetary value of these crops is included in an annual gross national product (GNP), economics is brought into this unit of study in the social studies.

Beyond correlation, the teacher may emphasise the relationship of more academic disciplines as compared to correlation, but less than in a problem solving procedure. This may be called the fused plan when the fused curriculum geography, anthropology, and political science (government) are taught as being related. Thus, in a social studies unit being taught, the teacher may stress a regions approach in geography such as in the Mediterranean area. Within this region, people speak diverse languages such as Arabic, and English among others. Different religions are in evidence, also, including Islam (Sunni, and Shiaas) as well as different Christian Orthodox churches. The languages spoken and religious beliefs adhered to stress the concept of "culture" in anthropology. Political science is also to be added to the scope of social studies learnings. Thus, the types of government which exist in the Mediterranean world nations will be studied by students.

In designing the curriculum then, the teacher needs to think of which plan of curriculum development to emphasise, be it the separate subjects, the correlated, the fused, and the problem solving or integrated approach. This situation involves planning the scope of any unit of study. A unit of study may then increase in scope in terms of the number of academic disciplines included such as in the following:

1. a single academic discipline such as history being taught as in Ancient History, the Roman Empire, the Middle Ages, the Renaissance, the Age of Kings, and Modern Europe, among others;
2. correlation with two curriculum areas being united, e.g. history and government; economics and history;
3. fused curriculum relating history, geography, economics, and anthropology;
4. problem solving with all academic areas involved as needed to solve a relevant, identified problem.

## Sequence in the Curriculum

Sequence emphasises the order of objectives to be achieved by students in class. It may also stress the order of learning opportunities to be pursued to achieve the stated objectives. A traditional approach in ascertaining sequence has been for the teacher to select the order of objectives and learning opportunities to be engaged in by learners. This tends to stress a strong teacher determined curriculum. The teacher may steer a rather straight course by implementing a separate subjects curriculum.

Toward the opposite end of the continuum, students with teacher guidance identify projects to work on sequentially. Here, the teacher works with students to determine criteria to use in choosing worthwhile projects. Once the project has been ascertained as being purposeful, students with teacher guidance need to plan the activity thoroughly. The plan must then be carried out to fruition. This takes interest and preservance. The learning by doing in a hands on approach is involved. Careful attention must be given to each step in the plan for its carrying out to completion. Standards for assessment of the project need to be developed and applied. This is also an important phase of the project method in that satisfactory evaluation is in evidence. It is salient to engage in each flexible sequential step of the project method such as in perceiving purpose, planning to attain the purpose, the actual doing of the project, and then its thorough assessment in terms of desired criteria. The project method of instruction permits much leeway for student input and its work. Students also do the assessing with their own crafted criteria. This is all done with the help of the teacher. The teacher is a guide and helper. He/she encourages, offers suggestions, but does not dictate how and what to do. Students are to become independent in decision making. These kinds of experiences will incorporate an integrated curriculum, since knowledge used depends upon the circumstances.

The in-between methods of curricular organisation—the correlated and fused curriculum—would emphasise degrees of teacher ascertaining of the curriculum as well as of learner input. Thus, the following situations in teaching might well accrue:

1. teacher led discussions of assigned readings;
2. students raising questions and selecting those to be answered with the use of a variety of experiences;
3. a combination of brief lectures and related hands on approaches in learning;
4. student/teacher planning of ongoing learning opportunities as well as of required work to be completed by learners;
5. cooperative assessment of student achievement involving learners and the teacher.

The above five enumerations tend to stress the correlated/ fused procedures of curriculum organisation. Thus, the teacher might well choose a separate subjects strand of instruction whereas students with questions to be answered would delve into knowledge from several academic disciplines.

## In Closing

Teachers, supervisors, and administrators need to do indepth study of different curriculum areas with the intent of making needed innovations. The objectives, learning opportunities, and the assessment procedures need analysis in terms of a separate subjects, an integrated problem-solving procedure, as well as in-between points of view. Student achievement is the key factor when making changes in the curriculum.

## REFERENCES

Banks, James A. (1997), *Educating Citizens in a Multicultural Society*. New York: Teachers College Press.

Curriculum Advice (1994), *Geography for Life; National Geography Standards*, Washington, DC: National Council for Geographic Education.

Emery, Donna W. (1992), *"Children's Understanding of Story Characters,"* Reading Improvement, 29 (1), 2-9.

Ediger, Marlow (2002), *"The Teaching of Social Studies,"* Edutracks 1(6), 6-11.

Ediger, Marlow and D. Bhaskara Rao (2001), *Teaching Social Studies Successfully*. New Delhi, India: Discovery Publishing House, Chapter One.

Ediger, Marlow, *The Holy Land*. Kirksville, Missouri: Simpson Publishing House, 1998.

National Council for the Social Studies (2001), *Curriculum Standards for Social Studies.* Washington, DC: NCSS, pp. 3-6. Excerpted from the Original by Walter C. Parker, and John Jarolimek.

Parker, Walter C. (2001) *Social Studies in Elementary Education*. Upper Saddle River, New Jersey: Merrill, Prentice Hall, Chapter Four.

Searson, Robert and Rita Dunn (2001), *"The Learning Styles Teaching Model,"* Science and Children, 38 (5), 22-26.

Wiggins, Grant (1993), *Assessing Student Performance: Exploring the Purpose and Limits of Testing*. San Francisco: Jossey–Bass.

# Issues in Organising the Curriculum

There is considerable debate among educators pertaining to means of organising subject matter for pupils to acquire. One may perceive the school/class setting as emphasising the separate subjects curriculum. In the separate subject curriculum, for example, the teacher may teach separate units pertaining to history only. Or, entire units of study may emphasise the social science discipline of geography. In attempting to relate content in the social studies, a teacher may teach diverse units of study correlating history and geography. Thus, historical events occurring in specific geographical regions is then being emphasised in teaching-learning situations. One may also perceive curriculum organisations as emphasising fusion of content. Thus, each social studies unit emphasises related content from the social science disciplines of history, geography, political science, economics, anthropology and sociology. To emphasises an integrated curriculum, further relationship of subject matter is needed. Thus, content acquired by pupils has lost its specific identifiable academic boundaries.

There are inherent assumptions in emphasising each specific plan of curricular organisation. These diverse plans in organising the curriculum will be discussed in the balance of this chapter.

## The Separate Subjects Curriculum

To emphasis a separate curriculum, the teacher may select educational objectives pertaining to one academic discipline for learners to attain. Thus, for example, in a selected historical unit of study, the teacher may write and emphasis the following goals for learners to attain:

1. The pupil will list in writing five causes of World War I.
2. The pupil will write a 100 word paper on the effects of World War I.

Each of these objectives largely emphasises content from the social science discipline of history. For learners to attain these goals, the teacher needs to select learning activities which contain historical content. Ultimately, the teacher may appraise if involved learners have acquired what is stated in the measurable objective.

There are numerous assumptions inherent in utilising the separate subjects curriculum. Among others, these assumptions include:

1. a separate subjects curriculum may truly reflects depth, rather than survey means of teaching and learning. If the teacher focuses largely upon one academic discipline in the instructional process, pupils may master specific content sequentially and in a comprehensive manner. Each academic discipline contains its own body of structural content for pupils to acquire. A watered-down curriculum occurs when teachers attempt to teach subject matter from several academic disciplines as being related. No single academic discipline receives adequate attention in the curriculum if subject matter from several academic areas is perceived by learners as being related;
2. each academic discipline contains its own unique sequence. In historical units of study, for example, pupils with teacher guidance may experience chronologically ordered events in space and time. Thus, in a study of history, pupils experience a selected order of vital happenings and events.

## The Correlated Curriculum

The correlated curriculum emphasises an initial approach in relating subject matter disciplines. Thus, for example, two academic disciplines may be presented by the teacher as being related. The following objectives, measurably stated might well illustrate correlation of content:

1. The pupil will list in writing five influences that geographical features had on battles fought during World War I. The social science discipline of geography is then correlated with history.
2. The pupil will write a 100 word paper on how productivity in five major nations, actively involved in battle during World War I, affected ultimate outcomes in this conflict. The social science disciplines of economics and history may then provide related subjects for pupils to acquire.

Advantages given for emphasising the correlated curriculum in teaching-learning situations include the following:

1. There are fewer separate subjects to emphasis in ongoing units of study when correlation as a concept is emphasised as compared to the separate subjects plan of curriculum organisation.
2. Individuals in society generally do not compartmentalise knowledge. Academicians tend to isolate/separate subject matter into component parts.

## The Fused Curriculum

The fused curriculum as compared to correlated methods increasingly relates content from diverse academic disciplines. Thus, each subject matter area in the social sciences can provide content for ongoing social studies units of instruction. The following pertain to specific goals involving fusion of content:

1. The pupil will write a two hundred word paper pertaining to seven causes, as a minimum, of World War II incorporating historical, geographical, political, economic, and cultural factors.

2. The pupil will list in writing five consequences of World War II. Consequences to be incorporated must relate to at least four social science disciplines.

There are selected positive marks given for stressing fused means in organising the curriculum:

1. Specialists in academic areas separate content into component parts. In society and life itself, individuals tend to synthesise content in order to solve problems.
2. Knowledge perceived as being related generally is retained for a longer period of time as compared to subject matter taught as being isolated or fragmented.
3. Borders, and boundaries between/among subject matter areas are not distinct but rather overlap. To divide the social sciences into component separate disciplines then becomes artificial rather than reality based.

## The Integrated Curriculum

The integrated curriculum emphasises problems solving experiences for pupils in the school/class setting. To solve problems, related context is utilised as diverse academic disciplines and life's experiences demand. Needed subject matter then loses its boundaries and borders with the framework of attempting to solve problems areas. Content from the social sciences, as well as from mathematics, science, language arts, music, art, and physical education are utilised as needed to achieve synthesis in problem solving.

Life in society demands that a person be able to solve personal and social problems. Thus, content must be perceived as being related by the problem solver. Problems need to be determined and the best solutions possible need seeking.

Gestalt psychologists believe that individuals initially perceive the whole of something rather than specific parts. It appears then that a viewer tends to perceive subject matter as being related rather than in terms of separate academic disciplines or fragmented knowledge. After introductory perceptions have been made, learners may then separate content as necessary to think critically and creatively. Selected academic disciplines might well be chosen to solve identified problems. This, of course, is pursued after wholeness (Gestalt) has been perceived in subject matter.

**In Summary**

There are selected questions which need answers pertaining to diverse means of organising the curriculum. One may perceive the problem in terms of points on a continuum. Toward either end, a point may represent the separate subjects curriculum. At the other end of the curriculum, a point may represent an integrated concept of curriculum development in which subject matter loses its boundaries and borders within a problem-solving framework. In between points on the line may represent the thinking of the correlated and fused curriculum. There are selected questions which need answering when resolving the inherent controversies.

1. Which specific curriculum area (e.g. social studies, language arts, mathematics, or science, among others) should emphasise: (a) separate subjects; (b) correlation; (c) fusion; or (d) integrated means in organising content from the academic world? Adequate rationale needs to be given to justify reasons given for organising content in each curriculum area in the school/class setting.

2. Which plan/plans of curriculum organisation might assist each learner to achieve optimally in intellectual, emotional, physical, and social achievement?

# 9

# Improving the High School Curriculum

Continuous criticism is made of the secondary schools of the United States. No doubt, any institution in society can be improved. The problem arises as to what needs to be changed and will the change lead in the right direction.

President Bush has advocated extending mandated testing to include the high school level, beyond exit testing. Presently students are experiencing mandated testing in grades three through eight and in grade ten. The new consideration is to test in grades nine through twelve. As yet, this has not become law. Will more testing improve student achievement on the secondary level?

## Reasons Given for Increased Testing

There needs to be a rationale for increased testing to include high school students. It does provide opportunities to notice if achievement is improving and taking place from one grade level to the next as revealed by test results. One problem here is comparing cohorts from one grade level to the next in terms of averages. Thus, the same students are not in each group being compared. Students are then being compared with a different group each school year. Selected educators emphasise the importance of the same students being followed through in measuring achievement through the high school grades. This stresses the value added procedure. It can then be noticed how a group of students fare in a longitudinal study. The same students then are being compared as they progress through the academic school years. Individual students might then also be compared in progress from one school year to the next.

A very significant question arises pertaining to what helps students to achieve well in school. The following are reasons given for doing much testing to assist optimal student learning:

1. it helps to pinpoint the teacher(s) who are not able to guide maximum student achievement. Accountability of teachers is of utmost importance;
2. students are motivated to do their best when they are tested to notice achievement;
3. measurable results are very specific and not subject to guesswork in interpretation;
4. well written tests secure the best information possible about student achievement;
5. parents obtain feedback on their offspring's progress by observing measurable results of learner progress.

There are a plethora of disadvantages in testing each year of student high school achievement. Time given to preparation for testing of students may be excessive. For example, in mandated testing students from grades three through eight, many teachers spend much time in drilling activities involving reading and mathematics. What is tested will be taught. There are many curriculum areas then that are slighted in teaching such as science, social studies, art, music, and physical education.

Second, a single test score from high school students limits the scope of what a learner has actually accomplished in a school year. The daily work of students is not included in the single test score. Third, for selected students, taking tests is not the preferred intelligence(s) possessed by a student. Testing involves the preferred intelligence of reading, whereas there are numerous additional intelligences for a student to use to show what has been achieved (See Gardner). Fourth, there might well be questions pertaining to the saliency of items on a test. The question arises, "Is this what truly has been beneficial for students to learn?" Knowledge items are being tested. Human relationships, citizenship, and caring behaviours are not being tested. Fifth, knowledge is one category of learning. There are also skills and attitudes which students should achieve to be successful in society.

Testing student achievement emphasises selected negatives, if used solely. There are penalties if students do not measure up. When students are being tested in different state mandated tests, they need to receive a passing score to go on to the next grade level. Also, the average mean score for the total school needs to meet adequate yearly progress (ayp). If a school fails to meet these standards two years in a row, it may be listed as "failing." The results of state mandated tests, called report cards, are published in the news media and are available for people to see. After three years of failing, the school/school system may be taken over by the state.

High school mandated testing, it implemented, needs to emphasise a balanced curriculum, not mathematics, and literacy only. The scope of testing needs to stress all relevant subject matter areas receive attention in instruction. Relevancy in what is tested in each academic area is significant. Trivia and the unimportant need to be omitted. Hopefully, a panel of experts and teachers in each subject matter field will be involved for extensive selection of content to be incorporated within a test for high school students. Recommended means of instruction should be appropriate for students rather than much drill for test taking. The following guidelines, which stress tenets of educational psychology, must be emphasised in teaching secondary school students:

1. the attention of students must be obtained for instruction with activities which obtain learner interests;
2. student meaning in ongoing lessons must be accrued so that learners understand that which is taught;
3. purpose needs to be established in any lesson so that students perceive reasons for participation in ongoing learning experiences;

4. motivated students achieve more optimally as compared to the unmotivated. Thus, these activities should motivate to provide a higher energy level for student learning;
5. individual differences need adequate provision since learners differ from each other in many ways.

**Styles of Learning**

Too frequently, all students are to learn from the same teaching materials and with the same methods of instruction. There are selected students who prefer formal seating arrangements as compared to those who prefer informal means. Some prefer more conformity in learning with teacher assigned materials as compared to those who wish the curriculum to be more open-ended for student choice of activities and experiences. Students also have preferences in studying by the self as compared to cooperative learning endeavours. Activities which involve sitting still as compared to those emphasising moving around in the classroom are further considerations. Using one sense in learning further complicates teaching in that some students prefer using visual, auditory, and kinesthetic activities while learning. Programmed learning in a step by step sequential programme appeals to selected learners more than an open-ended problem solving procedures, desired by others. Analytic learners as compared to global achievers need adequate provision. The former respond best to printed materials where separating facts from opinions, accurate from inaccurate statements, and the relevant from the irrelevant are separated. Global learners achieve best from visual materials of instruction (See Searson and Dunn).

With multiple intelligences theory, the teacher needs to provide more adequately for students who *reveal* best what has been learned through a multiplicity of developmentally appropriate methods. There are students who indicate in an optimal manner what has been achieved through verbal means as is true in reading. Testing situations do require much reading of test items. The following are additional intelligences of revealing learnings:

1. logical such as in reasoning. Mathematics emphasises much reasoning, but this skill is important in all curriculum areas;
2. musical/rhythmical as in writing lyrics and putting them to musical scores;
3. intrapersonal intelligences, such as achieving most optimally in individual endeavours;
4. interpersonal intelligence whereby these learners do best in group or collective endeavours;
5. bodily/kinesthetic in which learnings are indicated best through manual dexterity and physical prowess;
6. scientific intelligence whereby these learners do best in objective thought and thinking (See Gardner).

There are many variables that high school teachers need to consider when planning the curriculum of instruction. Worthwhile, quality objectives need to be chosen for students to achieve. These objectives need to incorporate relevant knowledge, consisting of vital facts, concepts, and generalisations. Additionally, there need to be skills objectives consisting of higher levels of cognition involving comprehension, application of knowledge, analysing subject matter content, integrating ideas, as well as assessment of content acquired. Also, quality affective ends need incorporation into the curriculum. Thus, good attitudes do assist students in achieving viable knowledge and skills ends. There are salient criteria to use in choosing objectives for student achievement:

1. Are the objectives significant for student achievement?
2. Would students be interested in achieving these objectives?
3. Is appropriate sequence involved when students achieve the desired ends of instruction?
4. Would learners feel motivated in achieving the stated objectives?
5. Is readiness in evidence on the part of students to attain the chosen objectives?

6. Would students feel the objectives to be relevant to attain?
7. Do the objectives make for a well rounded individual involving diverse academic disciplines?

## In Closing

There are a plethora of innovative approaches which have be attempted to improve the high school curriculum. Team teaching with its large group instruction, small groups, and individual endeavours has been tried and recommended. When first introduced in the 1960s, it still has adherents presently in high school instruction. A block of time schedule has also received much attention in the educational literature, but is largely considered as being another commendable idea in teaching and learning situations. Problem solving and inductive learning, also have their advocates. Both are noble goals to emphasise in high school instruction, among others.

New approaches in teaching must include creative selection of objectives, learning opportunities, and assessment procedures. The best curriculum possible needs to be in the offing for high school students.

## REFERENCES

Ediger, Marlow (1978), "Write on," *School and Community*, 65 (2), 12.

Ediger, Marlow, and D. Bhaskara Rao (2000), *Teaching Reading Successfully*. New Delhi, India: Discovery Publishing House, Chapter One.

Ediger, Marlow (1986-1987), "Reading Readiness and the Learner," *Minnesota English Journal*, 27 (2), 43-49.

Ediger, Marlow (1976), "Objectives and Oral Communication," *California English*, 12 (4), 7.

Ediger, Marlow (2001), "The School Principal: State Standards Versus Creativity," *The Journal of Instructional Psychology*, 28 (2), 79-83.

Ediger, Marlow (1999), "Teaching Reading in the Social Studies," *Aizona Reading Journal*, 26 (1), 15-18.

Ediger, Marlow (2000), "Speaking Activities and Reading," *Reading Improvement*, 37 (3), 136-144.

Ediger, Marlow (2000), "Writing, The Pupil, and the Social Studies," *College Student Journal*, 34 (1), 59-68.

Gardner, Howard (1993), *Multiple Intelligences: Theory into Practice*. New York: Basic Books.

Searson, Robert and Rita Dunn (2001), "The Learning Style Teaching Model," *Science and Children*, 38 (5), 22-36.

# 10

# Reflective Teaching in the Curriculum

Reflective teaching is receiving considerable emphasis in educational literature. What is reflective teaching?

Kumari (1994) stresses that reflective teachers are open-minded about which subject matter to use in teaching and learning situations. There is continuous evaluation by the teacher of vital facts, concepts and generalisations to be taught to pupils. What is taught is tentative and subject to change. Dogmatism and absolutism have no roles here to play in the selection of content to be taught. Rather flexibility is emphasised in selection of subject matter to be taught. Moral choices are made by teachers when selecting one objective as compared to another to be attained by learners. The teachers are responsible for actions taken. Relevance of objectives is of utmost importance. Decision-making is involved when the teacher chooses objectives for implementation. Immediate utility cannot be used as a criterion for choosing objectives, rather the teacher needs to evaluate the consequences when comparing the worth of objectives to be used in teaching/learning situations. There is purpose involved in the selection of objectives to implement in the classroom. Objectives chosen need to harmonise with the pupil's level of development in achievement.

Dewey (1913) clearly distinguished between behaviour that is routine as compared to that which is reflective. Routine behaviour is stressed through impulse, tradition, and authority. These behaviours are emphasised by teachers who do not reflect upon their work and lose sight of the purposes and goals toward which they are working. According to Dewey, reflective teachers are actively involved in teaching and are persistent in viewing the consequences of what is being done. Reflective teaching is problem solving.

Dewey (1929) raised numerous questions about developing a science of education. Among others, he raised the following:

What are the ways by means of which the functions of education in all its branches and phases... can be conducted with systematic increase of intelligent control and understanding? What are the materials on which we may draw and should draw in order that educational activities may become in less degree, products of routine tradition, accident and transitory, accidental influences?

There seemingly has to be change in order to update the curriculum. And yet, elements of stability are also salient. David (1995-1996) wrote the following pertaining to site-based management of schools:

Schools need a substantive framework within which to make appropriate choices. Whether that guidance is best communicated in the form of learning goals and standards, curriculum or content guides, or assessments is an open questions—as is the way in which choices about such guidance are made. The goal of site-based management is not to let a thousand flowers bloom nor to force every school in reinvent itself from scratch.

Reflection is then necessary to determine the amount of change necessary in moving from what is to what should be in the curriculum. A curriculum can be changed too frequently whereby teachers, administrators, and parents feel a lack of security in objectives being emphasised in teaching, learning opportunities to achieve the stated objectives, as well as evaluation techniques to ascertain learner progress. Tyler (1950) raised four vital questions pertaining to the curriculum which still are salient today and permits needed leeway to determine the amount of change desired:

1. **Which objectives should the schools emphasise in the curriculum?**
2. **Which learning activities should be selected to assist pupils to attain the desired objectives?**
3. **How should the learning activities be organised?**
4. **How should pupil achievement be evaluated to determine progress?**

Each of the above named questions requires time for deliberation and thought. The possible results of each decision made must be appraised. Creative thinking stresses individuals involved in making changes in the curriculum come up with new, unique ideas which truly would make positive changes in the curriculum. Problem solving in serious dimensions is certainly required.

## Problem Solving As Reflection

Experimentalism as a philosophy of education emphasises problem solving as a means of teaching and as a way of life. Experimentalism stresses that individuals cannot know the real world as it truly is, but the individual can experience only, the social and natural environment. Experimentalists emphasise a changing world, not one that is static or stable. Change abounds rather continuously. With change, new scenes and situations arise. Thus problems arise which need identification. Each problem is salient and relevant to the involved person(s). Problems that arise are vital and salient. Once the problem is clearly selected, the person develops an hypothesis, or an attempted answer to the identified problem/question. Problem selection and hypothesis development require reflective thinking. One then needs to reflect upon the problem as to its relevance. The hypothesis requires further reflection in that it must relate directly to the problem and be reasonable. Critical thinking is needed to separate vital problems from those lacking saliency. Critical thought also needs to be applied to the hypothesis in that it is important in reaching toward solutions to problems. Clarity in problem identification and hypothesis development is necessary. Otherwise, it is not clear as to what is being solved or what amounts to worthwhile solutions.

Reflective thinking is needed in evaluating the hypothesis in a lifelike situation. The experimentalist teacher is interested in the workability of the hypothesis. If the hypothesis does not work, a new one needs developing or the old one needs modification. Critically analysing the hypothesis is necessary here so that the hypothesis is appraised in terms of it having worked in the lifelike situation.

In reflecting upon problem solving, one can assess the problem area(s) identified or the hypothesis developed. Further reflection is inherent when the hypothesis is appraised or modified, if need be.

Flexible steps indeed are necessary in problem solving. There are no rigid processes, nor formal steps to follow. Inquiry-oriented paradigms of teacher education are emphasised when reflective thought is involved. Reflection becomes a part of teacher programmes.

Various models have been developed to encourage reflective teacher education programmes. Thus teachers think about and view experiences in teaching that have occurred with the intent of modifying and changing that which is deemed necessary. Weaknesses in teaching need identification as vital problems. Hypotheses need development to change that which needs modification. The revised approach in teaching is tried out in an actual teaching situation. It might be necessary to revise again or it might be the changed procedure is working well in teaching and learning situations. Teacher educators, teachers, and student teachers should reflect upon their teaching with the intent of making changes if necessary. The modifications can only be made based upon reflections on the act of teaching.

Ozmon and Craver (1990) wrote:

Since pragmatists are concerned with teaching children how to solve problems they feel that real-life situations encourage problem solving ability in a practical setting. Let us suppose that in a particular class some children want to devise an energy allocation system. This becomes the problem, and children may study plans and decide how they want to go about solving it. The motivation is there with student interest, and the teacher serves primarily as a resource person concerned with helping children get the maximum educational advantages out of the situation. But basically, the children do the work themselves, and they run into various problems about what kinds of allocation schemes to use, how to construct an equitable allocation basis, what social and economic issues must be considered, what possible alternative energy sources may be tapped, or how modern society could conserve energy better. It is in tackling such problems and try to provide solutions that children come to understand and control their own destinies better.

The above writers clearly state that pupils are to understand better what is being studied and learned. This indicates the need for careful reflection of the teaching act and its implementation by teachers.

## Decision Making Strategies

Existentialists stress pupils becoming proficient in the making of choices and decisions. A learning stations philosophy of teaching may then be implemented. Here, learners individually may choose which station and which task to work on. The pupil may select tasks which are individually oriented or collaborative endeavours. Choices made in terms of learning activities might involve problem solving or learning opportunities with non problem-solving experiences. The choice is up to the individual pupil.

There should be more tasks than what can be completed by any one learner so that omissions can be made of those tasks not possessing perceived purpose. Existentialist emphasise tasks involving the human condition of anxiety, tension, and dread. These are conditions that all people face in life. A curriculum could be built of the human experience using quality literature and history, among other academic areas. Within these curriculum areas, individuals make complex decisions in context as to what to learn. The teacher could also omit the human condition, in degrees (existentialism) and stress decision-making strategies only, so that pupils learn to select tasks from among alternatives. Additional objectives, learning opportunities, and evaluation procedures may also be planned through pupil/teacher decision-making.

Pertaining to the thinking of the late Carl Roger (1902-1987), a well known psychologist/philosopher. Webb and Sherman (1989) wrote:

Carl Rogers is an American Psychologist who had a major influence in his own field and in education. One could view his entire psychological theory as an attempt solve the problems of alienation and other directedness in modern society. He sees human interaction in this age as emotionless and unauthentic. Individuals may become overly sensitive to the judgements of others and typically live in a state of vulnerability. To protect themselves, Rogers believes they hide behind false fronts, dent their real feelings, and wall themselves from their emotions. Their efforts to conceal themselves are so great that they sometimes lose sight to who they really are. You will remember this that this form of alienation was called self-estrangement.

One's consequence of self estrangement, according to Rogers, is that individuals lose the capacity to fashion their own values. Individuals merely adopt the values presented by society. This is not necessarily a conscious process. Most people are not even aware of the values they inherit from the world around them. Such values may be contradictory or may not square with their personal experience. Under such conditions, Rogers says, values become rigid and are not easily changed.

**Reflections on Teaching**

What specifically are areas of teaching that teachers should reflect upon with problem solving involved to make necessary changes?

First, each teacher must reflect upon the quality of objectives emphasised in teaching and learning. Unless this is done irrelevant goals may be an end result. Time is a precious commodity in instruction and needs to be used wisely. One procedure to stress in using time wisely is to appraise the worth of each objective of instruction. Objectives for pupils to attain need to be vital and important. They should pass the test of scrutiny in being valuable for learner achievement.

Certainly, balance must be stressed among objectives to be emphasised. Thus three kinds of objectives need to be in evidence. These are knowledge, skills, and attitudes. Knowledge objectives should contain necessary facts, concepts, and generalisations for pupil acquisition. There is much subject matter for pupils to learn and the content to be stressed must be valuable for pupils to attain. Skills to be stressed in ongoing lessons and units of study need to place priority upon thinking analytically. Here, the learner should learn to separate facts from opinions, the salient from the not to salient, as well as reality from fantasy. Novelty of ideas need to be brought forth by the learner. These original ideas presented in an open-ended manner are needed from pupils so that improvements in life can be made from what is to what should be. Improvements come when individuals attain unique ideas to make necessary changes and modifications in society. Above all, problem solving should be a leading skill for all pupils to develop proficiency in. Unless problems are identified and solved, things cannot improve in society. Further skills for pupils to attain include attaching meaning to what is being learned, as well as using content and subject matter acquired.

Attitudinal objective are vital for learner acquisition. Teachers must reflect upon how well pupils are doing in achieving quality attitudes. Good attitudes toward learning assist pupils to attain knowledge and skills objectives more effectively. Thus pupils should develop appropriate appreciations, feelings, values, moral standards, beliefs, and standards in life. Unless pupils achieve worthwhile attitudes, optimal achievement is not possible.

Learning opportunities to achieve objectives may be multimedia or more limited use of media in teaching. The former may consist of videotapes, video disks, computer use, textbooks, trade books, dramatic experiences, writing prose and poetry for diverse purposes, oral communication activities stressing the utilitarian as well as the creative in expressions, internet and world wide web, among others. A school may not have these diverse kinds of media or the philosophy of teaching is that a more limited use of the different types of learning opportunities is best for pupil achievement. It comes as a surprise sometimes to selected teachers, administrators, and supervisors that a few instructors desire more limited use of media, for example, due to difficulties involved in harmonising their use with state mandated or locally determined ends. Then too, these instructors mention breakdown of technology, costs involved in its maintenance, and problems in balancing one's own classroom use of media with that of other classrooms. Whichever approach is used, media as learning opportunities need to assist pupils to attain worthwhile objectives, guide pupils to use their optimal achievement in learning styles, provide for diverse ability and interest levels, as well as encourage motivation among pupils.

There are several vital issues in arranging and organising content in each curriculum area. These are interdisciplinary studies versus a more separate subjects curriculum, thematic units versus more traditional means of organising the curriculum, psychological versus a logical sequence, among others. The best plan of organising the curriculum stresses that which assist each learner to attain as optimally as possible.

Evaluation of pupil achievement contains numerous problem areas requiring teacher reflection to determine which approaches are best to ascertain learner progress. Standardised norm referenced tests, teacher written tests, as well as criterion referenced tests have been traditional means of assisting learner progress. Newer procedures stress portfolio methods, contextual evaluation, performance standards, constructivism as a philosophy of teaching and appraising, as well as teacher written observations in terms of journal entries of pupil achievement within a given situation.

Methods of grouping pupils for instruction also need to be reflected upon to secure the best approaches in assisting optimal learner achievement. There is much debate among educators on the following:

1. grouping pupils heterogeneously as compared to homogeneously;
2. having full or partial inclusion of handicapped pupils;
3. learning stations approaches in grouping pupils in which learners individually choose the centre to work on sequential tasks be it individualised activities versus those in a committee setting;
4. stressing collaborative endeavours as compared to increased levels of wholesome competition among learners;
5. implementing departmentalised as compared to self contained rooms with block of time emphasis.

Much reflection needs to be in evidence to develop the best plan(s) of grouping pupils for instruction in the classroom setting. Mackinnon (1987) emphasis the importance of reflection as being the reconstruction of practical experiences. Here, the teacher assigns new salience to what has transpired in teaching. He/she especially perceives factors in practice situations previously unattended. The practitioner increasingly makes sense of practice situations. He/she then derives new implications for practice in the art or skill of teaching.

**In Summary**

What is a reflective teacher? A reflective teacher is one who combines the skill of inquiry with the attitude of openmindedness, responsibility, and whole heartedness. Further a reflective educator can critically examine his or her own actions, described a problem, generate possible solutions, and exhibit awareness of multiple perspectives. Hence these qualities are responsible to bring about change in the student and show an increase in scientific achievements. When the achievement of students in science taught by both the reflective and the traditional teachers were compared, there was an increase in the achievement of students taught by reflective teachers. Hence reflection is essential both for teachers' and students' achievement (Kumari 1994).

Toeffler (1990), who has done much writing in the area of futurism, emphasises the importance of self reflection in the work that has been done. With reflection upon completed work, one has a better chance of making improvements in future decisions and actions.

## REFERENCES

Dewey, John (1929). *The Sources of a Science of Education.* New York: Horace Liveright.

Dewey, John (1933) *How We Think: A Restatement of the Relation of Reflective Thinking to the Educative Process.* Boston, Massachusetts: D.C. Health and Company, Page 87.

David Jane L. (1995-1996), "The Who, What and Why of Site-based Management," *Educational Leadership*, Page 8.

Kumari, S.J. Shantha (1994). *The Relative Effectiveness of Reflective and Traditional Teaching on the Achievement in General Science of Ninth Standard Students.* Ph.D. Thesis, University of Madras, India, Page 194.

Mackinnan, A.M. (1987), *Conceptualising a Reflective Practicum in Constructivists, Science Teaching.* In Dissertation Abstract. International, Vol. 50, No. 12, June 1990, Page 3913 A.

Ozmon, Howard and Samuel Craver (1990). *Philosophical Foundations of Education*, Fourth Edition. Cincinnati, Ohio: Merrill Publishing Company, Page 141.

Toeffler, Alvin (1990), *Powershift.* New York: Bantam Books.

Tyler, Ralph (1950). *Basic Principles of Curriculum and Instruction*, Chicago, Illinois: University of Chicago Press.

Webb, Rodman P., and Robert Sherman (1989). *Schooling and Society*, Second Edition. New Edition: Macmillan Publishing Company, Pages 21-22.

# Philosophy of Teaching Mathematics

There are selected philosophies in the teaching of mathematics which can provide guidance to the teachers in developing the curriculum. Each teacher has selected concepts and generalisations which provide a framework for teaching and learning. A study of the philosophy of education may develop a reservoir from which the teacher may secure the background knowledge, attitudes, and skills to do a quality job of the reaching learners. Ozman and Craver (1990) wrote:

A study of philosophy of education seems imperative today, for we are in a critical era of transition. There has always been change, but seldom at our present accelerated rate, creating in many individuals what Alvin Toeffler has called the sickness of "future shock." In such an age, it is easy for people either to embrace more and more with little thought to eventual consequences or to resist change with little or no matter what. Educational philosophers, regardless of the particular theory they embrace, suggest that the solutions to our problems can best by achieved through critical and reflective thought. In one sense we can say that philosophy of education is the application of philosophical ideas to educational problems. We can also say with equal force that the practice of education leads to a refinement of philosophical ideas. From this viewpoint, educational philosophy is not only a way of looking at ideas but also learning how to use them in the best way. No intelligent philosophy of education is involved when educators do things

**simply because they were done in the past. A philosophy of education becomes significant at the point where educators recognise the need to think clearly about what they are doing and to see what they are doing in the larger context of individual and social development.**

## Idealism in Teaching Mathematics

Idealism is one of the oldest philosophies available which may assist the mathematics teacher to select objectives, learning opportunities, and evaluation procedures for pupils. Plato (427-347 BC) advocated idealism as a philosophy of education in ancient Athens. Above Plato's academy door, it stated that "no one is to enter unless they know mathematics." He believed mind to be superior to the body. Thus a strong academic curriculum in mathematics should be in the offing. Upon death, the mind/soul survives whereas the body decays. The mind must rule the body so that higher levels of choices are in evidence. It is the body that brings an individual to lower or inferior levels of choices and decisions. A study of mathematics assists the learner to attain well mentally. In the Forms (heaven), perfection is there in that a perfect something exists, such as different number systems, and geometrical figures, plain and solid. The here and the now on the changing earth is inferior to what is in the unchanging Forms. Thus a triangle, square, parallelogram, and circle, for example, in the here and now are imperfect models of what is perfect in the Forms. The same is true of all things and life on earth. What exists in the stable Forms is much superior to the world of change here on earth.

One only receives ideas about the Forms according to Plato. A person cannot perceived, the Forms as they truly are, but receives ideas through thought, mind, meditation, and intellectual endeavours. An idea centred mathematics curriculum pertaining to the abstract assists in achieving thinking individuals who reflect upon subject matter acquired. The well educated and the abstract thinkers have abilities to perceive or receive ideas pertaining to The Forms. Wisdom is a necessary prerequisite to perceive The Forms.

Idealism as a philosophy of education still receives much attention today. A mathematics teacher who is an idealist tends to emphasise mental endeavours as being superior to the physical and its emphasis. The mind is what is truly real about the person. Thus the mathematics teacher needs to stress pupils attaining abstract content in mathematics since this will aid mental development. Higher cognitive level objectives need to be selected and implemented in the mathematics curriculum. These objectives pertain to pupils being able to think critically synthesise content, and appraise what has been acquired. Mind is real and needs to be developed, according to idealism as a philosophy of teaching mathematics.

Concrete learning opportunities consisting of the use of real objects, and the semiconcrete emphasising use of illustrations, should be stressed only if they guide learners to understand abstract ideas in mathematics. The focal point of instruction is idea and mental development. One receives ideas of the natural and social environment only, not to replica of the real world. All informations are developed by the mind. Ideas are then secured about the natural and social facets of life. What is in back of this world is mind and spiritual, not the physical. Scope and sequence in mathematics emphasises mental and intellectual development of the pupil pertaining to the following topics:

1. base ten systems of numeration, estimating, as well as understanding positive and negative integers;
2. addition, subtraction, multiplication, and division on whole numbers, the integers, rational numbers, and irrational numbers;
3. geometry with its space figures, including plane (squares, rectangles, triangles, parallelograms, and circles, among others) and solid (spheres, cylinders, cones, prisms, and Platonic solids);
4. common and decimal fractions, as well as per cents;
5. measurement including linear, square and cubic;
6. graphs, tables, statistics and probability.

For the above named topics, pupils with teacher guidance need to study each in depth with emphasis placed upon learners attaching meaning to content being taught. Mathematics as general education is salient in developing mental maturity to work with numerals and number in the abstract. Critical thinking in the mathematics curriculum stresses mental development. Reason and intelligence are necessary to achieve fully in mathematics. The rational being then becomes increasingly mature mentally to use intelligence in dealing with the world of number and numerals. The teacher stimulates pupils to achieve using a variety of learning opportunities emphasising inductive and deductive methods of thinking. Idealists stress the concept of purpose for each human being in a purposive world. There is purpose involved in learning mathematics. The purpose involves, among others things, the development of the spiritual facet of the person. Human beings are not a part of the animal world, according to idealists. Rather they transcend that level and are endowed with rational powers that animals do not possess. Mathematics as an academic discipline can assist pupils to reach out from the finite toward the infinite in achieving intellectual and rational goals. Mathematical truths are *a priori* and thus have always existed. For example, any basic number sentence in mathematics such as $12 \times 10 = 120$ has always been true, prior to human experience. Each pupil must be guided by a competent and academically inclined teacher in discovering preexistent truths in mathematics.

For the idealist, mathematics presents content to pupils to encourage the development of reasoning persons in which the mind achieves in the direction of the Infinite, the unlimited in terms of attaining an ideal. Mind, not matter, represents ultimate reality. The mind and mathematics content stress reaching toward the Ideal or Infinite in achieving *a priori* content.

Since idealists in mathematics tend to recommend mental development of the learner as a major goal of instruction, a quality series of mathematics textbooks might well provide appropriate scope and sequence in the curriculum. The teacher's role here is to assist pupils to attain optimally in thinking mathematically. Brubacher (1966) wrote:

The most prolific writer on the idealist philosophy of education in the twentieth century was Herman Harrell Horne (1874-1946). At a time when idealism was fast fading as the dominant American theory of education. Horne managed to draw together the various strains of idealism into their more systematic educational exposition. In addition to much that is already familiar, he made two points of his own. One is his emphasis upon violation and effort in learning. The pupil is like the plant, he agreed with Froebel, in that his response is self active. But the child is unlike a plant, Horne continued, in that he can withhold his response. Hence the ultimate responsibility for getting an education rests on the will of the pupil. An education therefore is self education: it is the voluntary effort put forth by a self active mind. If effort is aided and abetted by interest, well and good. If not, then like Kant, Horne urged that the pupil in any case put forth effort in obedience to what he ought to do.

A second and more notable point in Horne's exposition is the fact that he did not make any significant alteration in the development theory of education in the light of the Darwinian theory of evolution, which was introduced to the world after the deaths of Hegel and Froebel. To be sure, Horne saw that evolution had made the developmental process irreversible and unrepeatable, in contrast to the Aristotelian pattern of matter endlessly reproducing the cycle of changes demanded by its form. The Absolute, however, had no difficulty in assimilating this new theory of development, for Horne could still say that the Absolute is; only the finite becomes. Pedagogically speaking, this seems to mean that through education the child still becomes in time what he was meant eternally to be.

Horne was a strong advocate of a subject centred curriculum. An idea centred curriculum in mathematics is then in evidence. The abstract numbers and numerals, the symbols of operation on numbers, as well as different formulas in determining area and volume, among others, might well provide a significant set of lessons and units in mathematics. Concrete and semiconcrete materials may be used to guide pupils to achieve well in the abstract.

**Realism and the Mathematics Curriculum**

The mathematics teacher who stresses realism as a philosophy of education believes in using the methods of science in teaching and learning situations. Objectives evidence, irrespective of the subjective person, is inherent in mathematics. Thus, subject matter in mathematics is true independent of the observer or person. Precision is a key word to use in teaching mathematics, according to the realist. A realist likes accurate descriptions of what exists. For example, he/she does not care for a person saying that the temperature reading in a room is comfortable. Rather, the exact temperature reading is wanted such as 22 degrees Celsius. If a person states that his/her blood pressure reading is normal, the realist desires to know the precise blood pressure reading using numerals for the systolic and diastolic readings. A teacher who emphasises that his/her pupils are attaining well does not satisfy the realist critic. Rather numerical results are wanted to ascertain how well learners are attaining, such as grade equivalents, percentile ranks, quartile deviations, as well as standard deviations from the mean and other derived or standard scores. Testing pupils to notice achievement is quite typical of the philosophy of realism. Thus, standardised norm referenced tests may be used to gather data on learner progress. Formative and summative tests are recommended to be given to learners to notice pupil progress in mathematics. The former is given to learners within an ongoing unit of study to monitor achievement along the way, as well as make needed changes in teaching. The summative test is given at the end of a unit of study in mathematics so that changes may be made, if evidence warrants, the next time the same unit is taught.

A mathematics teacher then who is a realist desires objectives of instruction to be stated in measurable terms, prior to instruction. The following are examples:

1. The pupil will add correctly ten number pairs, each containing single digit addends.

2. Given four geometrical figures, the learner will accurately compute the area of each.
3. The learner will change five common fractions to decimals and then to per cents.
4. Given three dimensional values for a rectangular prism, a triangular solid, a cylinder, and a pyramid, the pupil will compute accurately the volume of each geometrical solid.
5. Given data pertaining to the federal budget, the pupil will construct a line graph, a bar graph, and a picture graph.

For each of the above named objectives, pupils will reveal as a result of instruction if they have been successful in goal attainment. These objectives are stated with precision so that the mathematics teacher knows exactly what is to be taught. There is no guesswork in terms of what pupils are to learn. There are realists who advocate that the teacher announce prior to instruction what pupils are to learn as stated in the objective(s). Pupils then do not need to out guess the teachers in terms of what is expected of them as learners. When ascertaining how much pupils have learned as a result of instruction, the teacher receives numerical results such as the per cent of correct responses from a test of each pupil. The results from each pupil could also be computed to secure percentile ranks. Derived scores based on the normal distribution curve would indicate the number of standard deviations above and below the mean for each pupil.

A mathematics teacher who is a realist in terms of philosophy of education desires precise objectives for learner attainment. He/she matches the learning opportunities with the stated specific objectives so that an increased number of objectives will be achieved by pupils. What is in the learning opportunities then harmonises with what is stated in the objectives, no more and no less. Appraisal procedures harmonise with the objectives of instruction. Validity in appraisal is then in evidence. Results from the appraisal determine the number of objectives achieved satisfactorily by the learner. Results for the appraisal are objective in that independent of any evaluator, the number of correct responses would be the same each time. Subjectivity is then eliminated in the appraisal process.

Pertaining to realism as a philosophy of education, Bowyer (1970) write the following:

We have noted that there are different forms of naturalism and of idealism. The same is true of realism, which makes it difficult to pinpoint the distinguishing features of realism and to define the realist point of view. One element that the various forms of realism do have in common is a rejection or the idealist theory of knowledge that the various qualities of experience depend upon knower for their existence. Realists believe that the universe is composed of real entities that exist in themselves. These entities can be known, and their existence is not dependent upon a knower or perceiver. Although realists can argue on this point, they do not all agree when they attempt to build a metaphysical system. Here their views range from pluralism to dualism to monism.

The realist's epistemological views include epistemological monism where it is held objects are presented in consciousness, and epistemological dualism where objects are thought to be represented. The monists define mind as a relation between the organism and an object, while the dualist identify the mind more closely with the organisms. Realists do have a common tendency to view the world as the mechanism described by the physical scientists, and they generally believe in determinism, in orderliness in the universe, and in the objectivity of nature. The unifying theory of realism is that knowledge is thought to have a universal character and comes to man through his sensory capacity. The realists have confidence in their assertions about reality and value which is most discerning to pragmatists.

Since mathematics and its component parts are independent of any person, that is the content is objective and not subjective, precision and complete accuracy of answers to questions and problems are possible. Mathematics probably possesses the most objective subject matter as compared to other academic disciplines. This makes realism as a philosophy of education very useful in choosing precise objectives for pupils to achieve. The learning activities might well be aligned with the objectives and the appraisal procedures may be used to assess learner performance against the stated objectives.

## Experimentalism and the Mathematics Curriculum

The world of experience represents ultimate reality for the experimentalist. The realist believes that one can know the real world as it truly is in whole or in part. Also the real world exists independent of any observer or human being. The idealist believes that one can only know ideas about the real world, not as it is truly is.

With knowing what is experienced only, the experimentalist realise that change is all around us. Our perceptions change in time and place. Life in society continually changes. Thus problems arise which need identification. Each problem is life-like and reality based, not fictional. Clarity in problem selection is relevant. Vague, hazy problems do not lend themselves to solutions. An hypothesis is developed for the identified problem. The hypothesis is actually an educated guess or answer to the chosen problem. The hypothesis is not absolute, but tentative. The hypothesis is then subject to testing in a life-like situation. The consequences of the testing reveal the correctness or the lack thereof pertaining to the stated hypothesis. It is easy to understand how experimentalism with its problem solving situations is very relevant in ongoing lessons and units of study in mathematics. Problem solving is at the heart of the mathematics curriculum.

Problems should come from pupils in the world of society. Utilitarian problems are then identified, next textbook story problems. A practical mathematics curriculum is then in evidence. What is useful in the mathematics curriculum is desired in terms of objectives, learning opportunities, and evaluation procedures. The everyday experiences of people in society pertaining to mathematics provides content then for the experimentalist curriculum. Within a mathematics unit being studies, the learners choose problems to solve.

The experimentalist mathematics teacher needs to guide pupils to identify life-like problems. These are purposeful to the learner. The problems are useful to solve and have utilitarian values. Practical subject matter is then being emphasised in mathematics. The following represents practical problems for pupils to solve individually or within a committee setting:

1. In our school garden, how much of carrots, radishes, potatoes, and other crops should be planted? How much will the seeds cost?
2. How far apart should the rows be and how far apart should the plants be within a row?
3. What needs to be done to take care of the garden after the plants have come up?
4. Who will be responsible for each of the tasks in gardening?
5. Who will use the harvested crops? How much profit will we receive from the garden crops?

These among other problem areas will need to be solved in producing garden crops. New problems will emerge as the project is carried forward. There is much mathematics involved in establishing a garden for the school. Thus rows need to be measured as to length and distance apart. Space between plants will also need to be measured within each row. The cost of seeds needs to be determined. How much seed for each garden crop needs to be decided upon and implemented? Water needs to be used in selected amounts when rainfall is not adequate. Rainfall as well as water used for irrigation can be measured to determine volume. Time spent in taking care of the garden can be measured for each pupil. The amount of garden crops produced can be weighted. Perhaps, the produce will be sold. The price for each fruit or vegetable must then be ascertained. Produce items need to be weighted to determine the total price to be charged for the commodity. Time schedules for work for each learner should be completed. It is quite obvious that much mathematics is needed in the gardening project.

For the above example, there are selected principles of learning that experimentalism stresses as a philosophy of education. These include the following:

1. much planning by the involved group of pupils is needed;
2. mathematics is useful, not theoretical and abstract;
3. every day experiences in life provide content for the mathematics curriculum;
4. a learning by doing approach is emphasised;
5. pupils are actively involved, not passive recipients of knowledge, in ongoing mathematics lessons and units of study;
6. mathematics is not separated from life outside of school and is related to other curriculum areas, such as agriculture and food production, record keeping and accounting, physical education and in this case working in the gardening project, the language arts (listening, speaking, reading, and writing activities), science (such as under what conditions do plants grow best) and social studies (including economics and geography);
7. the pupil and the curriculum are not separate, but integrated entities;
8. the learner is heavily involved in curriculum development;
9. problems need identification and solutions;
10. social achievement is stressed in that committee endeavours are in evidence in the total project.

Experimentalism as a philosophy of education is a necessary component in mathematics since application of content is being emphasised. What is learned and acquired is used in life-like problem solving situations. The curriculum becomes and is utilitarian. The learner presently is actively involved in the useful and the utilitarian and does not wait for a future time to be a productive member of society.

There are additional situations in the school and classroom setting which provide experiences for learners in the mathematics curriculum. These are the following, provided as examples:

1. planning how a pupil is to spend his/her weekly money allowance;
2. planning objectives, learning opportunities, and evaluation procedures with pupils for sequential lessons and units in mathematics which stress practical experiences;
3. planning an experimentalist mathematics curriculum which harmonises with the National Council Teachers of Mathematics (NCTM) *Curriculum and Evaluation Standards for School Mathematics* (published by NCTM, 1906 Association Drive, Reston, Virginia 22091-1593);
4. planning how to divide cookies among a certain number of children who are involved in the lesson presentation. When teaching mathematics, there are numerous situations such as these, whereby pupils need to be actively involved in decision-making;
5. planning a class party related to a holiday in which mathematics is heavily used such as how many cookies, cup cakes, and soft drinks to purchase.

Mathematics teachers need to be creative in thinking about developing and implementing an experimentalist curriculum. There are numerous experiences which can be included in mathematics lessons and units of study emphasising the practical and the utilitarian in life-like problem solving situations. Atkinson and Malesks wrote the following:

> To a follower of Dewey, education has two sides—psychological and social; neither may be subordinated or neglected. The psychological nature of a child forms the basis for his education—it is the teacher's responsibility to make full use of his natural, spontaneous activities. Describing the original nature as being spontaneously impulsive rather than

passive. Dewey divided impulses into four kinds: the societal impulses, of communication or conversation; the constructive impulses to make things; the impulse to investigate things; and the impulses of artistic or creative expression.

With these impulses in mind, said Dewey, the school must be changed from a place for sedentary listening to one for active doing or working. The teaching processes must be planned to allow the child to learn wherever possible by his own experiences and, in that way, to acquire the habit of thinking. A proper solution to any problem demands intelligent thinking which becomes the principle factor in the ability to cope with new situations. Thinking as Dewey defined it is the use of the meanings of past experiences in interpretations of new situations.

Dewey felt that when the psychological and the social approaches to learning are separated, there is produced either a forced and external education in which freedom of the individual is subordinated to a preconceived notion of what society should be, or else a barren and formal development of the mental powers in which the learner has little idea of the use to be made of what is being learned. The school is primarily a social institution because its processes are basically no different from those going on continuously in life outside the classroom.

Therefore, Dewey claimed, the manner in which pre-school learning has been taking place should suggest to a teacher the physical and mental growth. The school ideally should be that form of social life into which can be concentrated those factors that most effectively cause a child to share the accumulated knowledge and skills of the race. Education can be considered as proceeding most satisfactorily whenever the individual is actively participating in social relationships with others.

## Existentialism and the Mathematics Curriculum

Existentialism stress the individual choosing and making decisions. To be sure, it is very salient that each pupil learn to engage in the making of choices. Life consists of making choices. Experimentalism emphasised also that pupils choose and make decisions, but usually within a committee setting. The belief exists in experimentalism that a pupil is a member of society presently and should be actively involved in the mathematics curriculum, but within a committee setting. Existentialism emphasises the individual as one who should determine his/her curriculum within a flexible framework. The teacher assists the pupil in achieving the latters goals.

I will mention a few other tenets of existentialism which may or may not apply to the mathematics curriculum. One first exist and then determines his/her essence. Thus the individual pupil should be heavily involved in determining goals, learning opportunities, and evaluation procedures in mathematics. I truly believe this to be a difficult method of teaching, but it certainly has its values and benefits. In all of teaching, it is the learner that is the focal point of instruction. Jean Jacques Rousseau (1712-1776) in his book *Emile* (see Brubacher, 1966) emphasised a one on one relationship between teacher and pupil. Thus a pupil would be taught by a mentor or teacher. Here, the teacher could truly provide for individual differences (one pupil and one teacher). The learner asks questions that would be of personal interest. The out of doors or nature provides the necessary curriculum for the pupil, according to Rousseau. The teacher then assists the pupil to find the needed information. Induction as a method of teaching is used here. The pupil does not need to depend upon other pupils for help in learning, but is to be an independent being, removed from the ills of society. Nor is the learner hindered in optimal achievement since no other pupil is there to hold the former back. The pupil does not need to gauge his (a boy in this case) learning against that of others in making comparisons. Uncomfortable comparisons between learners in achievement then can not be made in the one on one teaching situation. Rousseau's philosophy of instruction had definite tenets of existentialism. Which are selected mathematics experiences for pupils that Rousseau recommended?

1. estimating the height of a cherry tree so that an appropriate ladder may be found or made to reach and pick cherries;

2. measuring the size of boards to make necessary items and object.
3. becoming independent as a carpenter so that one does not need to be a servant of others. (Rousseau was very critical of norms in society). In being a carpenter, arithmetic and geometry are salient to learn within the framework of life-like situations.

Rugged individualism can be a term used to describe existentialism. Soren Kierkegarrd (1813-1855), a theistic existentialist advocated the person is first born and then finds his/her essence, meaning the individual must find his/his own purposes in life. These purposes or goals are not given to anyone, but must be found. The individual makes the self in an open ended universe, very limited in restrictions. Prior to this time, most philosophers stressed that the essences or purposes of persons were given to all first, and then the individual would be more certain as to what his/her role in life would be. Idealism was a prominent philosophy during the centuries and emphasised that the Infinite was ultimate reality and had purposes established for all. Kierkegarrd was a theistic existentialist who also believed that the Absolute was ultimate reality; however a long struggle was necessary in reaching this goal involving personal choices made. Jean Paul Sartre (1905-1980) emphasised atheistic existentialism as a philosophy of life. He also emphasised, as did Kierkegarrd, that an individual is born and then must find his/her own essence or purposes. With no Absolute, Sartre stressed that there is no one to manipulate the individual from above to determine purposes in life. Sartre's famous words that "Man is condemned to be free" certainly would make for a world of free choices for the individual. There are no absolutes.

Sartre (1971) in his essay "Man is Freedom," wrote the following:

It is strange that philosophers have been able to argue endlessly about determinism and free will, to cite examples in favour of one or the other thesis without ever attempting first to make explicit the structure contained in the very idea of action. The concept of an act contains, in fact, numerous subordinate notions which we shall have to organise and arrange in a hierarchy; it is to produce an organised instrumental complex such that by a series of concatenations and connections the modification effected on one end of the links causes modifications throughout the whole series and finally produces an anticipated result, but this is not what is important for us here. We should observe first that an action is on principle intentional. The careless smoker who has through negligence caused the explosion of a powder magazine has not acted. On the other hand the worker who is charged with dynamiting a quarry and who obeys the given orders has acted when he has produced the expected explosion; he knew what he was doing or, if you, prefer, he intentionally realised a conscious product.

This does not mean, of course, that one must foresee all the consequences of his act. The emperor Constantine, when he established himself at Byzantium, did not foresee that he would create a centre of Greek culture and language, the appearance of which would ultimately provoke a schism in the Christian Church and which would contribute to the weakening of the Roman Empire. Yet he performed an act just in so far as he realised his project of creating a new residence for emperors in the Orient. Equating the result with the intention is here sufficient for us to be able to speak of action. But if this is the case, we establish that the action necessarily implies as its condition the recognition of a "desideratum", that is, of an objective lack or again a negatite...

Stumpf wrote:

Whether they were theists or atheists, the existentialists all agreed that traditional philosophy was too academic, and too remote from life to have any meaning for them. They rejected systematic and schematic thought in favour of a more spontaneous mode of expression in order to capture the authentic concerns of concrete existing individuals. Although there is no "system" of existentialist philosophy, its basic themes can, nevertheless be discovered in some representative existentialist thinkers.

Existentialists believe strongly in conscious choices made by individuals as being desired. Moral judgement made in an atmosphere of freedom is a key concept stressed by existentialists.

An existentialist mathematics teacher needs to give learners as many options as possible in learning. The pupil chooses that option in a very open-ended mathematics curriculum. Most teachers of mathematics would tend to feel that existentialist philosophy is too free of borders and boundaries. Mathematics has its own scope and sequence. The scope and sequence has much agreement in and among mathematics educators. I would like do describe a mathematics unit which a few of my student and regular teachers have used. The approach I will describe emphasises the use of learning stations. The mathematics teacher here needs to decide upon the number of stations needed. Perhaps for twenty-five pupils, there should be at least eight stations. Each station must possess concrete, semiconcrete, and abstract materials of instruction. Also at each station, there is a task card which lists possibilities for pupils individually to choose from in terms of learning activities. The pupil may select which station and which tasks to work on sequentially. There should be an adequate number of tasks so that a pupil may omit that which does not possess perceived purpose. Sequence resides within the learner, not textbooks nor the teacher, in that the pupil orders his/her own experiences. If the pupil cannot find a station or task which meets personal purposes, he/she may plan with the teacher which learning opportunities to complete in mathematics. The learner is the chooser in deciding upon these tasks. The teacher encourages, assists, and guides the pupil in finding tasks and materials to complete that which has perceived purpose. Tasks at the different stations should have individual endeavours as well as those which stress committee work. The pupil then can work individually or with others, depending upon perceived purpose. In all cases, pupils individually sequence their very own learning opportunities.

There are mathematics teachers who stress additional tenets of existentialism in their teaching. The following are examples:

1. having pupils choose extra work to do in mathematics, beyond that which is required;
2. completing a contract with individual learners to indicate what he/she is to complete. The contract lists specifically what a pupil wishes to complete with a due date listed. What is in the mathematics contract represents that which the learner desires to complete with teacher assistance, not teacher education;
3. using teacher-pupil planning in the mathematics curriculum in which the latter determines what will be learned in sequence with instructor guidance. Thus the objectives, learning opportunities, and evaluation techniques are chosen by pupils with teacher guidance in mathematics.

Each of the above three enumerated items contains mathematics learning opportunities which can be incorporated into any classroom. To stress tenets of existentialism, the teacher must lean upon pupils in determining what they wish to learn. From within or intrinsically, the learner is the decision maker in terms of selecting objectives, learning opportunities, and evaluation procedures in the mathematics curriculum.

## In Closing

Four philosophies of teaching mathematics were discussed. Idealism stressed that pupils live in an idea centred mathematical world, but not an objective real world. Mental development of the pupil is a number one goal of instruction. The mathematics curriculum is viewed here as a part of the general education curriculum. Abstract content is prized higher that that which is concrete and semiconcrete. Ideas only can be known by an idealist. One only receives ideas of the real world of the realist. Ideas alone are also received of the experiences that experimentalists say can be known only. Realism emphasised that a person can know the real world in whole or in part as it really is. With pupils attaining precise measurable stated objectives in mathematics, they become more and more knowledgeable of the real world as it truly is. Each objective attained assists the learner in knowing more and more about the real world as it truly is, not merely ideas of this world. Bertrand Russell (Quoted in Wahlquist 1942) wrote:

The first characteristics of the new philosophy is that it abandons the claim to a special philosophic method or a particular brand of knowledge to be obtained by its means. It regards philosophy as essentially one science, differing from the special sciences merely by the generality of its problems, and by the fact that it is concerned with the formation of hypothesis were empirical evidence is still lacking. It conceives that all knowledge is scientific knowledge, to be ascertained and proved by the methods of science. It does not aim, as previous philosophy has usually done, at statements about the universe as a whole, nor at the construction of a comprehensive system. It aims only at clarifying the fundamental ideas of the sciences, and synthesising the different sciences into a single comprehensive view of the fragment of the world that science has succeeded in exploring.

Bertrand Russel was a mathematician and a philosopher. He believed strongly in two possible sources of information, mathematics and science. Why? These two academic areas alone provided empirical knowledge. The other subject matter areas, to Russell, were subjective and lacked reliability. Mathematics is precise and exact with its many patterns and formulas, according to Russell.

Experimentalism emphasises pupils learning that which is useful and utilitarian. Within a given problem area, mathematics is used to solved selected problems. Committee work is emphasised in that in society, people work in groups to solve problems areas.

Existentialism stresses individual choices made by a pupil in selecting sequential tasks and experiences in mathematics. The pupil is the chooser. The tasks may involve problem solving as well as other kinds of tasks.

The teacher needs to select that philosophy to implement which assists a pupil to attain optimally. Pupils differ from each other in numerous ways such as native abilities, past experiences, interests, motivation, and purposes. It behooves the mathematics teacher to prepare well and guide learners individually to attain optimally. Use of diverse philosophies of education to provide for individual differences should assist each pupil to learn as much mathematics as possible.

## REFERENCES


Atkinson, Carroll, and Eugene T. Maleska (1965), *The Story of Education*, New York: Chilton Books, 87 and 88.

Bowyer, Carlton H., (1970), *Philosophical Perspectives for Education*, Glenview, Illinois: Scott, Foresman and Company, 17.

Brubacher, John S. (1966). *A History of the Problems of Education*. New York: McGraw Hill Book Company, 128 and 129; 204-205.

Ozman, Howard, and Samuel Craver (1990). *Philosophical Foundations of Education*. Columbus, Ohio: Charles Merrill Publishing Company, xii.

Sartre, Jean Paul (1971). "Man is Free," As Quoted in *Introductory to Philosophy* by Tillman, Franklin A., et. al. New York: Harper and Row, 220, 221.

Wahlquist, John T. (1942). *Philosophy of American Education*, New York: The Ronald Press Company, 60-61.

Stumpf, Samuel Enoch (1971). *Philosophy, History and Problems,* New York: McGraw Hill Book Company, 455.

# Computer Use and the Mathematics Curriculum

**The number of computers in the classroom setting has increased much in the past few years. Reviews of software for computer use in mathematics reveal numerous deficiencies. Much needs to be done to increase the effectiveness of software and computer utilisation in the teaching of mathematics. This chapter will describe weaknesses in software for the mathematics curriculum. Proposed remedies will follow in the discussion.**

## Diagnosis of Problems

Software emphasising objectives in mathematics should not stray from significant ends in this important academic area. If an integrated programme is emphasised with another discipline, such as political science, significant learnings in mathematics for students may be greatly minimised. Proceducers need to realise that software emphasising content in mathematics needs to stress quality scope and sequence. The student may lose sight of valuable goals in mathematics, if an integrated curriculum is emphasised for its very own sake.

The writer would recommend that:

1. software stressing mathematics needs to contain vital learnings for students. If an integrated curriculum is inherent, adequate emphasis must be placed upon mathematics as being the core of subject matter presented;

2. other subject matter areas may then reflect the mathematics core learning. Appropriate breadth and depth of content in mathematics must be emphasised in the software.

A second deficiency in software content pertains to emphasising trivia. When students are asked to find the value of 5/7 of 93 = —, the viewer wonders if the programmer considers the concept of relevancy in programme development. Many major goals and objectives can be selected for students to attain. Would 5/7 of 93 = — be of these? The answer would be no. With the explosion of knowledge, it behooves the programmer to be highly knowledgeable of subject matter for, students to acquire in mathematics. The age-old question arises, "What knowledge is most worth?" This problem is still with us as it was with Hebert Spencer when in 1859, he wrote an essay on that exact title. It stimulate mathematicians and mathematics educators to seek and evaluate the most significant ends for learners to achieve.

The writer recommends for mathematics teachers and supervisors to:

1. engage in research to select vital goals and objectives for learner attainment. Basal textbooks comprising reputable series, filmstrips, films, and research study results might well provide background information for the ensuring research proposals developed by teachers and supervisors;
2. appraise current materials utilised in ongoing lessons and units. Objectives, learning activities, and evaluation procedures need to be assessed in terms of desired criteria.

A third weakness in software programmes emphasises that students must respond correctly the first time to a multiple choice item pertaining to subject matter presented on the monitor. Certainly, a student should have a second opportunity to punch in the correct command on the keyboard. To be sure, a student may merely guess at the first chance to make a response. Also, the second opportunity to respond might also involve a random guess. However, on the printout or on the monitor, it should show at the end of the programme how many first response items, as well as second chance answers, a specific learner got correct. Or, it will be revealed if a correct response was rarely obtained.

The writer would recommend that purchased software by a school district should:

1. provide opportunities for a second opportunity for learners to respond correctly within each specific programme involving drill and practice, as well as tutorial learnings. It can be highly technical in mathematics to make correct responses initially on any given programme. For example, in programmed items pertaining to decimal points in arriving at correct answer, the .1, .01, .001, and .0001 demand precision and exactness. Human errors can be made, even on the part of highly responsible students. When estimating is involved, a learner may well do more depth reasoning when given a second chance to make a response on the keyboard, as compared to a single response only;
2. emphasise clear subject matter in deductive or inductive presentations on the monitor, prior to learners responding in order to receive feedback on the response;
3. generate new questions to present content in diverse ways rather than the same subject matter and the same questions being asked in drill and practice or tutorial programmes.

Fourthly, excess time taken in loading with students are waiting to interact with a programme can be frustrating. Many software programmes have inherent excessive time given to the concept of loading. Certainly, mathematics teachers need to evaluate, if any one programme takes too much time in loading whereby the students, time is wasted and subject matter lack sequence. The writer has also wondered about the amount of time wasted in waiting for a programme to proceed in presenting subject matter on the screen so that appropriate learner responses can be made.

The following recommendations seem relevant:

1. subject matter in basal textbooks, workbooks, worksheets, and a laboratory approach in achieving may be more effective, as compared to programmes with the loading problem in mathematics software;
2. time on task research may well say that software selected for students needs to emphasise continual progress and achievement.

Fifthly, weak software fails to reward students for correct responses. If the reward appears on the monitor, it may be repetitious. Rewards in reinforcement need to be adequate and varied. The rewards should stimulate students to achieve at a more optimal rate. Reward reinforces a correct responses to encourage learners to achieve, attain, and progress.

The writer would recommend that rewards provided in software programmes need to:

1. encourage and motivate. Loud, distracting, rewards using peripherals should definitely be discouraged. Rewards should not be lavish to the point where an excessive amount of time is given in the programme to the concept of rewards;
2. be appropriate pertaining to the involved programme. Acknowledgement of correct responses is important. The rewards must be ample and sequential. They must be related to content in the programme. A lavish display of clowns, time consuming in nature, for each response correctly given by a student disrupts and is unrelated to the task at hand.

Sixthly, there are inherent problems in selected software in which timed tasks are involved. Slower achievers may not be able to respond to programmed items due to an extremely limited amount of time given. Certainly, a programme should emphasis what student can achieve. If too little time is given to read the content on the monitor and to respond, the software programme is self-defeating. Reasonable time limits must be available for students to respond within a specific time interval.

The writer recommends that software programmes be:

1. field tested adequately before they are put on the market for selling;
2. judicious in time provided for learner response. Let the involved student determine needed time to make each response on the keyboard.

Seventhly, software needs to contain interesting subject matter. All things being equal in stated goals, the more interesting the programme, the more likely it will be that students may achieve at a more optimal level in goal attainment. Interest is a powerful factor in learning. Boring content in software has no place in the mathematics curriculum. Subject matter needs to be stimulating and dynamic.

Pertaining to content in software, the writer recommends that:

1. programmers be aware of principles of learning from educational psychology and incorporate desired criteria therefrom, such as interest in student learning;
2. software on the market have prior testing in classrooms to determine if learner interest has been secured. A psychological curriculum in mathematics is in evidence if from the learner's, not the programmer's, point of view a programme provides set establishment.

### Criteria for the Selection of Software

Principles of learning from educational psychology have much to offer in guiding teachers in the selection of objectives, learning activities, and appraisal procedures. These criteria may well be utilised in the choosing of software in the mathematics curriculum.

As a first principle of learning, students need to experience interesting subject matter in computer activities. Software needs to secure the attention of learners. Boring content will not facilitate the student in attaining desired mathematics objectives. Establishing set or getting learners to attend to ongoing lessons and units is vital. Mathematics teachers need to try out software, prior to its being purchased, to notice if involved students are interested and to achieve vital goals.

A second principle of learning advocates students being actively involved in a programme. Each student needs involvement in making sequential response to a stimuli. If learners merely absorb information from the monitor, passivity in learning is involved. Rather students individually need to respond to subject matter presented on the monitor. After acquiring content, the learner must answer questions pertaining to ideas attained. Feedback may then be inherent in providing the students information about the correctness of the response.

Thus, learners need to respond frequently to subject matter presented in each programme. Based on the response, feedback to the learner is a must.

Meaningful content needs to be presented to students. With meaning attached to subject matter being pursued, students understand what has been taught. It is indeed unfortunate if a student does not attach meaning to content being read on a monitor. Certainly, to be useful, subject matter must be on the understanding levels of students. Success in learning comes about when the learner understands what has been learned and is able to achieve sequentially.

Success on the part of each student is important when pursuing a software programme. With carefully prepared programmes and tested in pilot studies, learners should be successful approximately ninety per cent of the time in responses made in a programme. Quality attitudes within learners may well be enhanced with successful experiences in the mathematics curriculum. Developing an adequate self concept is important on the part of each student.

Students also need to perceive purpose for learning. Reason should be inherent when pursuing a programme. A lack of motivation for achieving may accrue when a student fails to sense reasons for participating in a mathematics programme. Reasons need to be stressed to students to participate be it anyone of the following kinds of programmes:

(a) *Drill and practice*. Reasons for experiencing drill and practice need to be experienced to the learner. A deductive approach is then emphasised. Or, the teacher may wish to utilise an inductive procedure to have learners perceive values in experiencing drill and practice programmes.

(b) *Tutorial*. New sequential subject matter in mathematics is emphasised with tutorial programmes. Success in learning here is enhanced when content is based upon previously acquired subject matter.

(c) *Games*. Enjoyment of gaming approaches may stimulate selected students to achieve more optimally in mathematics. Two to four pupils generally can be provided in computerised games. Wholesome competition needs to be in evidence among participants. Easier items in mathematics to respond to earn fewer points per item as compared to increasingly difficult questions. Thus, there could be four levels of complexity of responses to questions pertaining to mathematics content. Easy items answered correctly could receive 5 points. Increasing complex items may receive 10, 15, and 20 points sequentially. If students are evenly matched for the game, much learning can accrue within a quality learning environment.

(d) *Simulations*. With life-like experiences, problem solving and higher levels of cognition can truly be in evidence within the framework of simulate content in software. Several learners generally will be involved in simulation or role play activities. Feedback to each decision made by a learner must appear on the monitor.

(e) *Diagnosis and remediation*. Quality software in diagnosis should pinpoint very specifically the kind of errors made by a student. Models on the screen should be shown what is correct procedure would be to remedy the identified deficiency.

(f) *Computer managed instruction (CMI)*. Checking answers on computerised answer sheets of students is a very useful, time-solving approach for teachers to use to appraise learner progress. The printout should clearly point out how many students missed each test item.

Feedback might then be given to the teacher in terms of the quality of each test item, as well as success in learning on the part of pupils.

Grades for each student can also be stored on a computer. CMI has many practical uses for the teacher of mathematics.

**In Closing**

Software and microcomputers have a significant role to play in assisting students to achieve well in mathematics. Weaknesses in software and computers need to be identified and remedied. Technology must assist learners to achieve optimally on an individual basis. Computers and software, as audio-visual aids, should be utilised to guide each student to achieve as much as possible in mathematics.

Positive headways have been made in attempting to develop quality software for students in mathematics. There still are long strides to make to analyse and remedy the identified deficiencies. Mathematics educators, educational psychologists, as well as programmers must harmonise efforts in securing the best programmes possible for learners. Software should not be developed for the sake of doing so. Rather, each programme must assist students to achieve mathematics proficiency. Drill and practice, tutorial, games, simulations and remedial programmes need field testing and necessary modifications prior to their use in the classroom. Problem solving in school and in society needs to be an ultimate goal in the teaching of mathematics. Life consists of identifying and solving of problems.

# Helping the Child in Mathematics

Mathematics can be a very practical area of knowledge for pupils. In every day events, people buy goods and services in which money is used. Addition of the total amount of goods when purchased is necessary. If cash is used, the change needs to be determined from, for example, a twenty dollar bill. Subtraction is involved here. It seems that whatever a person does in society, number is involved with its basic four operations of addition, subtraction, multiplication, and division.

There is much the parent can do to assist the child to do well in mathematics. Lets us look at this from the point of view of informal situations in ever day life. The child should go along to the grocery store. Here the child notices items placed in a shopping cart. The parent should discuss with the child the cost of items purchased. Those that are easiest to understand by the pupil should be discussed first. How these purchases are paid for should be noticed by the child, such as cash, by check, or credit card. In visiting a hardware store, the parent may purchase a hammer. The child needs to notice the cost of the hammer, as well as of other goods purchased. The child needs to notice the bar code on each item, and the computerised receipt after the item(s) have been paid for.

Prices of cereals may be looked at on boxes at breakfast time and discussed with children. By doing this, children become increasingly conscious of how important mathematics is in every day life.

Parents, too, will want to assist their children at home in mathematics so that better achievement is in the offing in school. It is important that parents have knowledge of what is been emphasised presently in mathematics by looking at the schools web site. Then too, if the pupil brings home the mathematics textbook and work sheets from school, the parent has a better idea of how to help the learner. If the parent does have access to these materials, he/she has guidelines to use in working with the child by reading and following ideas in the textbook.

The most important point to make in teaching mathematics is that pupils are able to make sense of what is being taught. When pupils are learning to count, they should first be able to say the numbers correctly in the proper order. Next, after the pupil can count to ten or twenty, he/she needs to count by using one to one correspondence in counting objects. The child's finger should touch the first block and say "one." This is followed by touching and the second block and saying, two," and so on. It is important to touch each block separately and say the appropriate number. The child is counting discrete objects such as blocks. In addition to blocks, the child may count pencils, books, children, and pens.

Second, the pupil should be encouraged to learn to add. Encouragement is a very silent practice in the psychology of education. The parent may say in a sincere manner, "I am sure you can add the following," or "This will be easy for you." Put downs and rude comments should never be made. Thus, two pencils may be counted. If the child can count two pencils in the first set and three in the second, he/she can count five pencils when the two sets are joined together. The number sentence 2 + 3 = 5 should be written down to show the child the written equivalent. The order of pencils may be switched by counting three pencils first then two pencils. Together the new set has five pencils. It does not matter how the two sets are ordered, the child discovers that 2 + 3 or 3 + 2 = 5. That the order of addends may be changed and it does not affect the sum is important for the child to understand. This is called the commutative property of addition and can be used continuously no matter what the size are of the addends. Thus, for example,

329 + 246 = 246 + 329. Children need to learn the commutative property of addition at a young age since it always will be helpful.

Third, understanding what is being learned is so important. If pupils understand what addition is and they see the meaning of it being shown with blocks, they will be ready for more complex learnings as feedback indicates. Feedback from pupils tells the parent how the pupil is thinking and what is being understood. Parents should not move forward to new learnings if a child, for example, does not understand what 2 + 3 =. Have the child first learn what 2 + 3 = before moving on to something new. Memorising something which is not understood is detrimental to a child's future learning. New learnings are based upon the old in mathematics achievement. Thus, if pupils have learned meaningfully the addition facts to five as the answer, they should then be ready to do subtraction. If a child has learned that 2 + 3 = 5, he/she may be ready to learn the inverse operation such as 5–3 = 2 and 5–2 = 3. Blocks may be used to show the child that five blocks take away three blocks leaves two blocks, or five blocks take away two leaves three blocks. The parent should use a variety of materials in teaching subtraction such as plates, erasers, sheets of paper, playing cards and dice. It takes time for the young child to master a subtraction fact meaningfully such as 5–3= 2. The parent needs to make sure that pupils do understand subtraction of each fact before moving on to a new learning.

Fourth, pupils need to be rewarded for doing well. A parent may say, "That's good," if the children answers or thinks correctly. "That's good," is a reward. To vary the reward, the parent may pat the child on the back for responding well in mathematics. Generally, these kinds of rewards should be adequate. There are parents and teachers who give physical prizes as rewards for a child doing well such as giving candy, gum, or an inexpensive prize. Usually, a pupil needs to know ahead of time what to do to obtain a reward. The parent can say to the child, "If you answer correctly two out of three times to an addition problem, you will receive a piece of candy." The reward is obtained after the child has fulfilled what is desired by the parent. What is desired needs to be reasonable and there is a good chance the child will be successful in its doing. There are those who do not agree with the giving of physical rewards for learning and the author is one of these. Learning should be done because it is enjoyable and the child inwardly wants to learn.

Fifth, once pupils have gain proficiency in basic addition and subtraction facts, they should be assisted in understanding place value. If 5 + 4 is added, then 9 which is the total may be shown on a place value chart. Nine congruent (same size) slips of paper may be placed in the one's column of a place value chart. If 9 + 1 is added, then one slip of paper should be placed in the ten's column and zero slips of paper in the one's column since 9 + 1 = 10, with zero ones and one ten. As time goes on, pupils may learn to show place value on a place value chart with larger values. The numeral 26 would have six congruent slips of paper in one's column and two slips in the tens column (two tens equal twenty). Six plus twenty equals twenty-six. A larger value such as 345 would have five congruent slips of paper in the ones column, four slips in the tens column, and three in the hundreds column.

Sixth, children should be helped to learn by discovery methods. Discovery methods emphasise the joys of finding out on one's own. This is opposite of the parent telling the child how to add to how to subtract. Although, there are times when it is very appropriate to do so. But, as much as possible, the child should be helped to find out on his own. Why? Most of us need to do this when being adults. There may be no one there to assist us. Any how, the child needs to become as self sufficient as possible and lean upon the self. How can the parent help the child to learn by discovery? Let us assume the child now has learned the initial basis of addition and subtraction and now multiplication is to be introduced. The following may be stressed in sequence:

- how many blocks are in this set? The assumption, here is that there are two blocks in the set.

- how many would there be if I had twice or two times that many? Words need to be used which children understand. It may be necessary to show the child another set of two blocks to indicate two times that number in the original set. The child needs to understand what 2xs means. Go over this slowly and meaningfully with the child and notice problems which the child has in understanding multiplication.
- the number sentence $2 \times 2 =$ needs to be written clearly for the child to see. He/she can then associate the 2xs the number of blocks on the table. The child might then discover that $2 \times 2$ is the same as $2 + 2$. Multiplication is repeated addition. The parent may use other numbers to help the child in beginning multiplication. For example, the parent places one block on the table. The child may be asked how many blocks there are on the table. Now the parent may ask how many there are if 3xs the original one are to be considered. The 3xs may be counted with the child in terms of one, two, three. These basic understandings are always the same. If $283 \times 7$ are to be multiplied, the understandings are consistent. Thus, 7 times 283 =. It would be a lengthy process to have 283 objects shown seven times on a table. A large table indeed would be needed here. But with meaningful foundational learnings, the child, when ready, can multiply $7 \times 3 = 21$, $7 \times 80 = 560$, and $7 \times 200 = 1400$, then $21 + 560 + 1400 = 1981$. This is shown presently merely to indicate that with the understanding of place value, learnings can be understood by the child. Readiness is an important factor which indicates these learnings would come at a much later time.

Seventh, library books should be read aloud to pupils involving arithmetic. There are fascinating library books on this topic which children enjoy. When ready, they may join in on the reading of these books as the child and the parent read together its contents. Reading together makes it possible for the child to read aloud, even though some of the words are not identified correctly. in a psychologically sound environment.

The topic of division may arise in the literary selection. For young children, division will need to wait until interest is shown and a desire to learn its content is in evidence. There are young children who are highly precocious and do ask questions about mathematics and its four operations of addition, subtraction. multiplication and division. Division is related to multiplication in that it undoes an answer. If $4 \times 2 = 8$ and this is easy to show with four members in a set and two of these sets are wanted, then dividing by four is two and eight divided by two is four. The parent may show this by taking eight blocks and dividing them into two equal parts. There are then four members in each set. Eight blocks may also be taken and divided into four equal sets of two members, when eight is divided by four.

Library books on mathematics may provide a springboard for children increasing their interests in mathematics. Interest is a powerful factor in the child's motivation to learn mathematics.

## Organisations to Foster Children's Interest in Mathematics

There are numerous organisations which have been formed, generally under the auspices of the school, to help children in mathematics. Parents have then organised a mathematics club. Here, parents decide upon a mathematics topic to pursue. Generally, the agreed upon objectives will pertain to methods of home teaching. One group determined objectives to pursue on teaching carrying or regrouping to young children. Teaching aids were made to help the child visualise the regrouping process. A place value chart was made by each parent in the group with pockets to show the ones, tens, hundreds, and thousands columns. Coloured construction paper was cut using a paper cutter for making congruent slips of paper, for the ones column, and different colours for the other place values— 10s, 100s, and 1000s. Another set of parents made fraction cut outs to resemble pies divided into eighths, sixths, fifths, fourths, thirds, and halves. These were used for the young child to identify fractional parts and also to notice equivalent fractions. Thus six eighths were place over three fourths of a pie to notice equivalent fractions. A third set of parents made flannel boards with felt cut outs to use in teaching mathematics in the home setting. The cut outs usually were made to reasonable animals. Thus, a parent may place on the flannel board five felt cut outs and join this set with three more. The child is then asked how many members there are with the two sets combined. The inverse operation may also be taught, "If there are eight felt cut outs on the flannel board and three are taken away, how many are left?"

In the mathematics club questions were discussed pertaining to what parents found useful in helping the child at home in mathematics achievement. A newsletter may be developed with an editor appointed or elected to announce the decided upon date, time, topic(s) to be covered, and place of the next meeting. Purposes of the meeting should also be included in order to encourage increased attendance of parents.

Parent/teacher conferences are a good time to ask the teacher questions about assisting the child at home to achieve well in mathematics. The parent should write these questions down at home, prior to attending the conferences. E-mail messages may also be sent to the teacher when needed, to ask for assistance in home tutoring or to discuss the overall progress of the child. This is a quick and economical way of conferencing with the teacher.

Summer school sessions can offer the child an enriched mathematics curriculum. The sessions therein will have established objectives for pupils to achieve. Varied learning opportunities will be available to assist pupils to achieve the objectives. Evaluation techniques should be used which help in ascertaining if the stated objectives have been achieved by pupils. The home tutoring by the parent should synchronize and relate directly to the summer school programme in school mathematics.

After school tutoring programmes are available which should assist pupils to develop vital learning in mathematics.

These programmes should assist pupils to achieve more optimally in mathematics. The home tutoring programme should reinforce children to achieve the mathematics objectives of the tutoring programme.

The home and the school need to work together for the good of the child in mathematics. When these efforts are harmonised, better achievement will be an end result.

# Homogeneous and Heterogeneous Grouping in Reading Instruction

The reading teacher needs to use grouping procedures, which will assist each pupil to achieve, as well as possible. A single plan is not adequate. Dogmatically adhering to one approach may emphasise an agenda of the teacher, writer, or speaker, rather than guiding each pupil to do as well as possible in reading.

## Flexible Plans of Grouping

There are plans of grouping in which it does not matter if homogeneous or heterogeneous grouping is involved. Individualised reading is an example. Here, a pupil chooses, from among alternatives, which books to read sequentially. A variety of topics need to be available as well as library books on different reading achievement levels. The learner may have a conference with the teacher after a library book has been completed.

With the use of experience charts, either heterogeneous or homogeneous grouping may also be used. Here pupils, based on an experience such as objects on a learning centre, provide ideas for the teacher to record on the chalkboard or with the use of computers. Ideas come from learners, not from the teacher. After the content has been recorded by the teacher, pupils orally read aloud the recorded ideas as the teacher points to each word. The experience chart may be reread orally as often as necessary. Here, pupils develop a basic sight vocabulary and enjoy actual reading activities.

Grouping of pupils with experience chart use may be either homogeneously or heterogeneously grouped. It may not matter, only slow learners may hold fast learners back from more optimal achievement.

Basal reader use in a heterogeneously grouped classroom may find learners on a variety of achievement levels read the same story with high achievement levels established. Peer grouping might be used to assist slower achievers "catch up" or attain the determined levels of reading achievement. In peer grouping, the fast reader might be held back while assisting the slower learner in reading.

Homogeneous grouping of pupils places the top achievers in one group, the middle achievers in a second group, as well as the slow readers in a third group. These three reading groups are formed within a heterogeneously grouped classroom. There are reasons for grouping homogeneously for reading instruction within a heterogeneously group classroom:

1. Each group; collectively, may achieve as optimally as possible.
2. No group is held back due to slower achievers within its group.
3. The fast achievers may motivate each other in the fastest group of the three.

A major reason given for heterogeneous grouping is that faster readers may assist the slower achiever in reading. However, the fast reader may be giving up time here in pursuing his/her own goals in reading. The gifted/talented also need a reading curriculum which was developed to assist optimal achievement.

Perhaps, a balance can be struck between the gifted/ talented reader helping slower readers to achieve, as well as pursuing a purposeful, personal reading curriculum.

## Grouping Homogeneously by Classroom

Pupils may also be grouped homogeneously by classroom with the top achievers being in one classroom, the average in the second, and the slowest in the third. The following are always salient when grouping learners for instruction:

1. Be respectful and accepting of all pupils as having extreme worth.
2. Show a feeling of "I care for you and want you to do well," for all pupils.
3. Avoid group names such as robins, bluejays, and starlings.

Flexibility needs to be a key concept in all plans of grouping. Thus, a pupil may be achieving more rapidly and needs to be placed in a higher achieving group.

Homogeneous grouped classrooms should not be frowned upon when they assist pupils to achieve as optimally as possible. Grouping should be used as a means of helping a pupil to learn to read as well as possible. The self-concept should be improved upon as a result of the group the child is in for reading instruction. No pupils should be held back from achieving optimally on an individual level. A major goal of teaching and learning is to guide individual, optimal achievement, not to follow an agenda in what an educator feels in democratic or equality. Individual, optimal achievement also needs to be emphasised in social or collaborative settings, challenging to each pupil regardless of ability levels. No pupil should be held from becoming the best reader possible with the intent being to provide for "equality." Equality has to do with providing quality in instruction so that each pupil is:

1. Prized highly
2. Recognised for contributions made, regardless of abilities possessed.
3. Valued in any group setting.
4. Praised and has esteem needs met.
5. Achieving growing, and developing well.

Regardless of the kind of grouping used, the negative can occur, such as:

1. Ridiculing and belittling pupils.
2. Rudeness in working with others.
3. Impatience in relating to pupils and teachers.
4. Hostility and hatred in the social arena.
5. Partiality to a selected group.

Homogeneous versus heterogeneous grouping of pupils for reading instruction will not guarantee that the above five named negative behaviours will be minimised. A particular kind of grouping will not eliminate pupil behaviour, such as looking upon others or being segregationist in thinking. Rather, attitudes and beliefs need to be changed so that all are important, teachers and pupils alike, in the social kingdom.

## Criticism of Homogeneous Grouping

There has been much unwarranted criticism of homogeneous grouping of pupils for instruction. The negative criticism has zeroed in on the following:

1. Education becomes "elitist" if top achievers are grouped homogeneously. Why should it be "elitist" if the top achievers achieve as optimally as possible. It is undemocratic if these pupils are not given the best instruction possible, as should be done for all pupils.
2. Talented/gifted pupils should be in heterogeneous groups so they can help slower readers catch up.
3. Slow readers have no role models unless there are gifted/talented to set the pace for more optimal achievement.
4. Homogeneous grouping does not close the gap between fast and slow readers. Somehow, closing this gap is democratic. The reasoning here is fallacious. Should better readers then be held back to close the gap?
5. Research states that all pupils achieve better in collaborative endeavours with heterogeneous

grouping. *Even if* a study indicates that pupils in heterogeneous/collaborative groups do better than pupils in homogeneous groups, at the .05 level of significance, there are still 5 out of 100 that do not do better. Anyway, the quality of each research study needs to be evaluated. Most "research" studies have too many loopholes to be useful.

## In Closing

There are plans of reading instruction that can incorporate either heterogeneous of homogeneous grouping. With programmed reading, using textbooks or computers, each pupil achieving individually, ideally as rapidly as possible. The pupil sets the pace for tutorial, diagnosis and remediation, gaming and simulation programmes.

The Big Book approach may stress either plan of grouping. Of course, selected pupils will and do achieve more rapidly than do others.

The ideal in grouping pupils for instruction is optimal achievement for each.

# Foundations of Primary School Mathematics

Primary school mathematics teachers need to emphasise basic ideas in mathematics which provide a foundation for future pupils achievement. Laying of the foundation for primary aged pupil provides a basis for attaching meaning and understanding in successive lessons and units of study. Learners might then feel increasingly more secure that what is being learned also has value for ensuring content to be acquired. Thus subject matter being stressed in an ongoing lesson or unit of study in mathematics will provide a framework in experiencing new content, being related to that which has been achieved. Pertaining to teaching second grade pupils and intervention, Schmidt wrote the following involving her research:

In planning interventions for students, the connection between assessment and instruction can provide useful information to remediate students' concepts and skills. This action research study suggests some classroom strategies to assist in providing intervention. They are: build on students' conceptual and skill understandings, use developmentally appropriate games and activities, and organise classroom learning centres to manage group and individual intervention experiences in the classroom.

Thus, foundations of mathematics instruction should build on what pupils know and can do rather than having pupils attempt to achieve a remote goal that is impossible to attain.

Ediger (1994) wrote the following pertaining to what teachers should emphasise and what pupils need to experience:

1. *Meaningful lessons and units of study*. With meaning, pupils understand and comprehend that which was contained in ongoing learning opportunities.
2. *Interesting content and skills in the curriculum*. With interest, the pupil and the curriculum become one, not separate entities. Pupils attend and achieve from ongoing lessons and units.
3. *Purpose in learning*. With purpose for learning, pupils accept reasons for attaining relevant facts, concepts, and generalisations presented...
4. *Sequence in learning*. With quality sequence, pupils relate newly acquired content with that previously achieved Previous knowledge attained provides readiness for the new objectives to be achieved...
5. *Balance among objectives stressed*. Thus knowledge, skills, and attitudes—three kinds of objectives need to be achieved by pupils. These objectives interact are not in isolation from each other. For example, if pupils possesses positive attitudes, they should achieve knowledge and skills more readily.

**Foundations of Learning**

What should be emphasised in mathematics objectives which provide a basis for understanding sequential facts. concepts, and generalisations? Primary grade pupils need to experience a hands on approach in teaching. The hands on approach needs to stress that which is reality in society. Real live problems need solutions. Diverse concrete materials need to be in the offing to represent the lif-like situations and related solutions. A variety of pictorial representations should be used simultaneously or directly after the concrete phase of pupil learning.

We will now deal with symbolic representations for primary grade pupils of the concrete and pictorial phases of instruction. If upper primary grade pupils are studying the value of 3 x 2 represented by the concrete and the pictorial, they need to see a variety of settings whereby symbolic notation is written on the chalkboard or appears on a monitor/printout from a personal computer The second symbolic notation also needs to be experienced and seen by pupils such as $2 \times 3$ (the commutative property of multiplication).

Second, pupils need guidance to read 3 x 2 as "three times two" and 2 x 3 as "two times three." Mathematics has its own vocabulary which pupils need to read, master and understand. Role learning and memorisation are not to be emphasised unless pupils attach meaning to what has been learned.

Third, pupils with teacher guidance need to read and write the addition number pair of $3 \times 2$ and $2 \times 3$. For the former, the addition form is 2 + 2 + 2, whereas the latter is 3 + 3. If pupils do not understand the addition forms as they relate to multiplication, they need to receive assistance using concrete and pictorial methods of learning Quality sequence is always important in mathematics teaching and learning.

The inverse operation of multiplication which is division also needs meaningful emphasis such as "6 divided by 2" as well as "6 divided by 3".

Fourth, pupils need to experience reading and writing the words of "three times two" as well as "two times three." There is a definite mathematics vocabulary that pupils should be able to understand, read, and write. Reading achievement in mathematics is just as important as reading in any other academic discipline.

Fifth, learners need to attach meaning to set concepts. Thus pupils with teacher assistance need to understand the concepts of "3 sets having 2 elements each" as well as "two sets having 3 elements each." Set notation needs to be written correctly by pupils as sequential learnings accrue. Drawings may be made or pictorial forms observed on monitors of computers by pupils pertaining to each of these two different sets.

Sixth, arrays should be experienced by pupils. Diverse media should be used to guide pupils to understand an array. Thus the following, among other illustrations, should be meaningfully taught to pupils:

| | |
|---|---|
| * * * | * * |
| * * * | * * |
| | * * |

Seventh, number lines may be used to communicate mathematical idea. The number line can be located on each pupil's desk as well as a large number line should be placed on the wall for all pupils to see clearly. Pupils individually and in a group may observe and work with numerical concepts and generalisations when using a number line. Pupils may then notice the following:

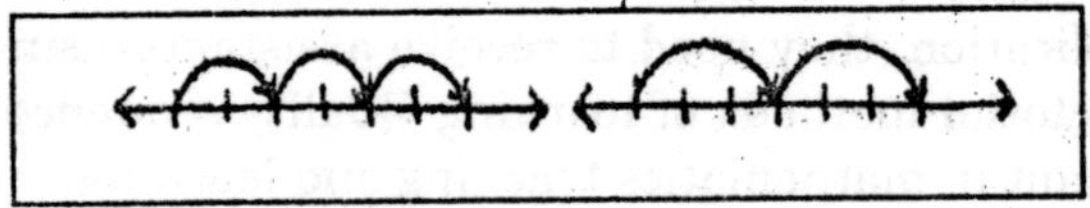

Eighth, pupils should see and understand ordered pairs and how they are written. Thus pupils need to attach meaning to the following:

(3.2) (2.3)

In sequence pupils may experience more complex concepts and generalisations, pertaining to each idea presented in this chapter.

Ninth, in sequence and with quality achievement, pupils need to understand vital vocabulary within a number pair such as the following in multiplication:

| | |
|---|---|
| 3 factor | 2 factor |
| 2 factor | 3 factor |

Tenth, learners need to experience problem solving, critical thinking, and creative thought. The problem solving model should stress pupils identifying a problem or perplexing question, information needs to be secured in answer to the problem or questions, a hypothesis should result as a possible solution or answer, and the solution/answer needs to be tested in a lif-like situation. Critical thinking requires separating accurate from in accurate information, relevant from irrelevant content, as well as plausible from nonplausible subject matter. Creative thought, emphasises stressing the new and the novel in mathematics. Originality of ideas and processes developed by pupils stresses creative thought.

## In Closing

Pupils need a framework from which to operate in the mathematics curriculum. The framework provides background information for pupils when participating actively in ongoing lessons and units of study. Readiness for learning new facts, concepts, generalisations, as well as processes provides learners with prequisites to work on goal attainment. A structure is then needed to accommodate and assimilate what is new in terms of knowledge, skills, and attitudinal objectives. If pupils learn to use meta-analysis, they might well monitor more effectively their very own progress. With meta-analysis, pupils think about how they learn. For example, what happens when the pupil engages in problem solving? The individual learners thinks about and rehearses what is essential here. Thinking about thinking or how one makes discoveries in problem solving emphasises situations pertaining to meta-analysis.

Pupils then need to experience foundational ideas pertaining to the mathematics curriculum. We have attempted to present foundational ideas for later primary grade pupils, as an example. Objectives for primary age pupils should be achievable and yet challenging.

Pertaining to an effective mathematics curriculum. Kennedy and Tipps (1994) wrote the following:

Effective teaching requires that teachers develop lesson plans that are more than lecture and recitation. Research into the ways children learn and research on the methods and strategies that enhance learning provide a basis for making instructional decisions. Use of many concrete manipulatives, active involvement of pupils in exploring and generalising mathematical principles, organising cooperative learning groups, and attention to developmental needs of different learners are practices that teachers should include in planning lessons and learning activities. Teachers who employ such techniques report with satisfaction how much the children understand and how excited they are about learning mathematics. Teachers must also refer to state or district goals and objectives in developing activities. Goals and objective such as those stated in the NCTM's *Curriculum and Evaluation Standards for School Mathematics,* guide planning for a variety of learning activities in a well-balanced mathematics programme.

Pupils may work individually as well as in cooperative learning situations. They may experience the separate subjects curriculum or increasingly achieve objectives which stresses more of an integrated or multidisciplinary curriculum. Gender equity should be valued in that both boys and girls need to achieve optimally. Multicultural education needs incorporation in that pupils from diverse cultural groups are respected and accepted so that quality teaching in mathematics is available for all pupils. Staff development of primary grade teachers is a must! These teachers need to incorporate in their teaching that which assists primary pupils to secure a value foundation for learning.

What is learned on the primary grade levels has significant implications for pupils achievement as each one makes continuous progress.

## REFERENCES

Ediger, Marlow (1994), "Early Field Experiences in Teacher Education, *College Student Journal,*" 28: 302-303.

Kennedy, Leonard M., and Tipps, Steve (1994). *Guiding Children's Learning of Mathematics.* Belmont California: Wadsworth Publishing Company, Pages 38-39.

Schmidt, Mary Ellen (1995), "*Mathematics Intervention: Second Grade Place Value Concepts*", Education, 116: 232.

# 16 Mathematics-Social Studies Making the Connections

Much is written and spoken about the interdisciplinary curriculum. Thus, educators are recommending that more and more subject matter from diverse academic disciplines be taught as being related, rather than as isolated entities. Toward the beginning of the twentieth century, pupils were taught in a manner whereby each academic discipline remained as being separate, not integrated. There were an increasing number of educators who recommended that content be correlated whereby two academic disciplines were taught in an integrated manner. Later, about the 1930's, more and more educators were recommending that borders and boundaries be minimised among different subject matter areas. John Dewey (1859-1952) was a strong exponent of problem-solving in the curriculum. Here, pupils guided by the teacher would identify a problem, gather data or information in answer to the problem, develop a tentative answer to the problem, and test the answer in a life-like situation. Problem-solving did not emphasise a specific subject matter area. Rather whatever was needed to solve that identified problem was used as information. John Dewey was a very early advocate in the interdisciplinary curriculum. Already in 1896, he established a laboratory school connected with the University of Chicago. Pupils in this school used problem-solving procedures continuously as learning activities. The teacher assisted learners in problem-solving. Teachers did not lecture to pupils nor did the latter sit at desks in a passive manner.

Rather pupils were actively engaged in selecting and solving lifelike problems. Dewey emphasised that problems be life-like and related to what exists in society.

Problem-solving strategies are difficult to emphasise in teaching, but these approaches do stress an interdisciplinary curriculum. Whatever content is needed to solve problems is used, regardless of the academic discipline involved. What does a complete interdisciplinary curriculum do to scope and sequence in mathematics? Mathematics educators seem to have considerable agreement on what should be taught in the curriculum. Thus scope and sequence can be spelled out more clearly and with considerable agreement among educators as compared to the other academic areas taught in school. On the other hand, educational psychologists have long recommended that pupils perceived knowledge as being related, not as isolated entities. Thus if a pupil perceives the relationship of knowledge among diverse academic disciples, he/she might be able to recall content better due to one known idea being related to another idea, and so on. A learner perceiving knowledge as being isolated may not be able to think of related content in a lesson or unit of study. He/she perceives content in terms of isolated entities, unrelated to the larger whole.

## Relating the Mathematics and the Social Studies Curriculum

We have supervised student teachers and regular teachers in the public schools for thirty years. These teachers have tended to work as a term. Many of the ideas we will be presenting here come from supervising teachers in the public schools. Teachers have used slides and other visual aids in the Middle East to relate mathematics and the social studies. We will now explain a few examples of slide content to the world of mathematics.

1. The wall around old Jerusalem is two and one-half miles in length and is forty feet tall. Here, teachers have had pupils mention landmarks that are two and one-half miles from the local school building. Sometimes teachers have checked pupil responses by driving to the landmark mentioned after school hours. Since the wall of Jerusalem is about forty feet

high, comparisons are made with the height of the local school building. The height of the local school building is generally available in the principal's office. Proportion has also been used to determine the height of the local school building such as noticing the length of its shadow and comparing it with the height of a stick and the length of its shadow.

2. a second slide shows the city of Jerusalem which has an elevation of 2,500 feet. Learners find out the elevation above sea level locally. Comparisons are then made of the elevation of Jerusalem with the local area. Many times pupils have wanted to compare the degrees in latitude of Jerusalem with the local area.

A third slide shows the city of Jericho with its luscious fruits and vegetable crops grown. Pupils wonder why Jericho can grow an abundance of garden crops and yet be classified as a desert with less than eight inches of rain per year. Research is done by pupils with teacher guidance to notice that the rain has fallen in Jerusalem from the clouds by the time it reaches Jericho. Jerusalem being 2,500 feet above sea level and Jericho being 800 feet below sea level, in a distance of eighteen miles, has the Judean hills in between. The winds blow westward from the Mediterranean Sea to Jerusalem and most of the rain is deposited near Jerusalem before reaching Jericho eighteen miles east. The moisture laden winds leave the Mediterranean Sea (at sea level) and rise to an elevation of 2,500 feet at Jerusalem. As the moisture laden winds rise, cooling occurs and rain falls. Cool air cannot hold moisture as well as does warm air. As a wind go further to Jericho, there is a very little moisture left in the winds that originated in the Mediterranean Sea.

Here, pupils have studied the affects of elevation and the amounts of rainfall in a given area of the world by discussing and solving problems such as the following:

1. How does elevation effect rainfall amounts in the Dead Sea area as compared to nearby Jericho?

2. Why are these two areas desert in nature with less that eight inches of rainfall per year?
3. How is irrigation water secured for making Jericho a beautiful garden spot?
4. What landmarks do you know that are eighteen miles apart, such as is the case of Jerusalem and Jericho? Estimation is involved in hypothesizing and each hypothesis may be checked out if necessary.

There is much emphasis placed upon using arithmetic when solving these problem areas.

To bring it closer to home base, numerous pupils have been on Pike's Peak, just outside of Colorado Springs, Colorado. This peak is 14,500 feet in elevation above sea level. Learners have studied and solved problem areas such as the following pertaining to Pike's peak:

1. How does the temperature reading on this peak compare to its base? Why does this occur?
2. What happens to animal life as the altitude increases when going upward to Pike's Peak on the cog railway or by hiking?

A fourth slide on the Middle East area of the world stresses the Crusaders capturing the Holy Land area, especially Jerusalem and Bethlehem. This occurred in 1099 AD during the First Crusade. Pupils are fascinated with determining how many years ago that was. There are other relevant dates that interested pupils in finding out the number of years that have since elapsed such as:

1. Constantine and his mother Queen Helena building the first Church of the Holy Sepulchre inside the walled city of Jerusalem in 330 AD.
2. Justinian the Great building the Church of the Nativity in Bethlehem in 529 AD, which still stands today.
3. The building of the present wall around Jerusalem in 1542 by the Ottoman Turkish Empire.

Pupils individually become fascinated in comparing their very own age with the number of years that have gone by since the inception of each of the above incidences.

A fifth slides shows gasoline prices as indicated by Israeli currency and the liter unit used to sell gasoline. Learners wrote story problems involving the purchase of a certain number of liters of gasoline purchased involving shekels, the currency used per liter purchased.

A sixth slide shows population of the following nations of the Middle East: Jordan, Egypt, Israel, Lebanon, Saudi Arabia, Iraq, and Iran. Here, pupils in committees developed a bar graph showing the population of each of these nations. Statistics can be taught at an early age and not at the graduate level of instruction only.

A seventh slide shows the capitol city of each Middle East nation mentioned above with the related population. Respectively, these capitol cities are Amman, Cairo, Jerusalem, Beirut, Riyad, Baghdad, and Teheran. Pupils used these data to make a line graph in comparing population figures of capitol cities in the Middle East area of the world.

A eighth slide shows the number of people in the Middle East who belong to the following religious groups: Sunni Muslim, Shia Muslim, Judaism, Christianity, and Alawite Muslim. Learners in committees developed a circle graph showing the per cent of members in each group of the total number for the entire set of members. This activity is suitable for talented fifth and sixth graders as well as those who are highly motivated to learn in mathematics. All pupils should be challenged to achieve as much as possible in mathematics.

An eighth slide shows a map of the West Bank, Jordan, and Israel. Pupils were to ascertain the number of kilometers as well as miles between the following given cities:

(a) Hebron and Jerusalem

(b) Bethlehem and Nablus (ancient Samaria)

(c) Beersheba and Nazareth

(d) Petra and Amman

(e) Tel Aviv and Eilat.

A ninth slide shows replicas of people, building, and religious symbols made of olive wood, mother of pearl, and different metals. Prices are given in shekels. Learners computed the price of each item in US currency.

A tenth slide contained the Mosque of Abraham in Herbron, the Church of the Holy Sepulchre, as well as the Western Wall of the ancient Jewish Temple in Jerusalem. Pupils were given the following dimensions:

1. an inch equals four feet. Each committee of pupils determined the length, width, and height of the Mosque of Abraham, using the actual size of the building on the slide;
2. a centimeter equals one meter. Pupils in cooperative learning were to find out how long, how wide, and how high the Church of the Holy Sepulchre and the Western Wall are, using the size of the buildings/ structures on the slide to obtain dimensions for the scale drawings.

For each of the tasks above, pupils felt motivated and encouraged to pursue and achieve. We did not see any wasting of time on the pupils' part. Pupil purpose appeared to run high in perceiving connections between mathematics and social studies.

Interest was also extremely high when pupils studied the ancient Egyptian system of numeration when studying Egypt in the Middle East. The Egyptian system emphasised the following:

1. A single tally mark or stroke for a value of "one." There could be as many as nine tally marks to show units or values of one each. For example, a value of two would have two tally marks; three would have three tally marks and so on.
2. For a value of ten, one arch, also called a hoof of a cow, would be drawn. Nine arches had a value of ninety.

3. A coil of rope had a value of 100. Thus two coils of rope equaled 200; three coils = 300; and four coils of rope equaled 400, and so on. Ten coils of rope equals a lotus flower.

4. Each drawn lotus flower had a value of 1,000. Two lotus flowers had a value of 2,000 whereas three lotus flowers had a value of 3,000, and so on. Ten lotus flowers equals a bent finger.

5. Each drawn bent finger had a value of 10,000. For each 10,000 value, one bent finger was drawn. Two bent fingers equal a tadpole.

6. Each tadpole had a value of 100,000; thus in showing a value of 700,000 seven tadpoles need to be drawn. Ten tadpoles equal an astonished man.

7. Each astonished man had a value of one million, the number of millions that needed to be shown on paper were the number of astonished men drawn.

Pupils enjoyed activities pertaining to the Egyptian system of numeration when provided with a certain number of drawings and then asked to provide the base ten equivalent. For example, a drawing consisting of two astonished men, six tadpoles, three bent fingers, five lotus flowers, one coiled rope, eight arches, and four tally marks has what value in base ten? The answer is 2,635,184. Learners felt that much thinking went into the determinations of the value of the drawings when using the Egyptian system of numeration. Certainly, pupils need to be ready for activities such as the Egyptian system of numeration before being activity engaged in these kinds of experiences. If pupils are ready, they do appear to have much interest in other numeration systems than base ten.

The Roman system of numeration is more practical as compared to the Egyptian system in that the former is seen at selected places today. They are clocks, corner stone block in buildings, and wristwatches that contain the Roman system of numeration. Pupils read time in the school hallway, from a clock with Roman numerals. The local school building contained the date of the corner stone laying CMLXI or 1961. To be sure the Roman system as we know it has changed a little since the days of the Roman Empire, approximately 2,000 years ago. However, I recommended using the symbols as are commonly shown in society. I believe pupils appreciate base ten more so after studying a system which does not have the order or patterns that base ten has. Learners realise from a study of the Romans system of numeration that:

1. it uses an additive system in writing values such as a value of three has 3 tally marks; 3 X's has a value of thirty with each X having a value of ten.
2. it has a subtraction system in writing numerals such as CM = 900. The symbol "M" equals 1,000 and the smaller C value of 100 indicates subtracting the latter, amount from 1,000.
3. there is no place value in the Roman System of numeration.
4. it is difficult or impossible to add, subtract, multiply, or divide, as is done in base ten, using the Roman system.

Pupils should be challenged to make as many discoveries as possible involving different systems of numeration.

**In Closing**

It is possible to have pupils relate mathematics to social studies. Pupils might well be encouraged to achieve objectives in mathematics when perceiving that it is related to social studies.

We believe strongly that interest in learning is a powerful factor in learning in mathematics. Thus the attention of pupils need to be secured in order for learning to take place. Teachers need to choose those learning opportunities which will guide learners to perceive knowledge as being related. Learners need to apply what has been learned to new situations. The level of application in learning assists pupils to perceive reasons or purpose for learning. Thus what is/has been learned can be used in diverse situations. Generally, knowledge that is related can be applied sooner than that which is unrelated.

# Improving the Science Curriculum

Each person lives in a world of science. The natural environment affects all of us. It operates in terms of scientific theories, principles, and laws. Pupils in the public school setting need to achieve relevant goals in science. These goals should be attainable, meaningful, and possess purpose for the learner. To improve the quality of life for each person, a problem-solving approach should be emphsised in ongoing lessons and units in science. With problem solving, change occurs from what is to what should be in science.

Diverse schools of philosophical thought will be discussed and how each might relate to improve the science curriculum.

## Realism in the Science Curriculum

A science teacher who is a realist emphasises that one can know the real world, in whole on in part, as it truly is. The mind then does not modify or change what is being perceived. Tillman, Berofsky, and O' Connor (1971) wrote. "Most people when they think about the objects of perception, would say that they perceive a world of objects which is external to them and which exists independently of their perception of it. This view is called realism."

Since the external world is perceived the way it is in actuality, specific objective of instruction can be determined by scientists and science educators for pupils to achieve. Each objective must be relevant and is a part of the whole that can be known by the learner. Thus in geology, biology, chemistry, physics, and astronomy, among other academic disciplines, measurably stated objectives of instruction need to be emphasised in teaching and learning in the science curriculum. With quality learning opportunities selected by the science teacher, pupils either achieve or do not achieve the specific objective(s) as a result of instruction. Measuring pupil achievement in learning stresses what pupils have learned that was stated in each objectives. Realists desire observable results in learning from pupils. The results are verifiable regardless of which teacher is appraising learner progress. The verification principle is very important to teachers of science who adhere to realism as a philosophy of instruction.

Skinner (1979) was a leading advocate in stressing precise objectives for pupil attainment. Reinforcement is emphasised to reward correct/good responses in learning. Observable, measurable results are obtained from what pupils have achieved. Guesswork is not involved, but per cents, standards deviations, quartile deviations, grade equivalents, and percentile ranks emphasise how well each pupil is doing in the area of science instruction. Numerical results of pupil achievement in science is wanted by the realist teacher. Scores from tests; objective evaluations of science experiments and demonstrations performed by pupils; rating given to learner performance as well as responses to questions, oral reports, portfolios and related papers written in which interobserver reliability is in evidence, present data as to how well pupils are achieving. These procedures qualify as objective means of appraising learner progress.

Mager (1972) stressed the importance of writing objectives so they are operationalised. Objectives are then specific and clear to teachers, pupils, and other interested persons. Learning opportunities may be chosen and aligned with the stated objectives. Appraisal procedures used in determine pupil achievement are also aligned with the objectives. Quality validity and reliability are then in the offing. A pupil reveals if he/she attained or did not attain a stated objective. The realist science teacher wishes to know if pupils individually are or are not achieving objectives of instruction. The results may then be reported to parents in a very precise way.

Prior to instruction, the teacher may announce to pupils which objectives will be emphasised in the science lesson or unit. The pupil knows exactly what will be expected in terms of knowledge or skills to be obtained. The involved pupil should have more confidence in learning when realising what the instructor's expectations are. The science teacher might desire to arrange the objectives in an ascending order of complexity. A logical sequence follows since the teacher sequences objectives in science for the pupil to achieve.

Advantages given for emphasising realism as a philosophy of instruction are the following:

1. teachers may realise how successful they are in teaching since results form pupil learning are clear and observable;
2. objectives, learning activities, and evaluation procedures are interrelated in that the learning activities and the evaluation procedures must harmonise with the stated objectives. Thus, for example, it becomes easier to choose learning activities than otherwise would be the case due to the harmony needed between these activities and the stated objectives;
3. effective schools research states that pupils achieve better if there is a clear relationship between the learning activities and the evaluation procedures with that of the objectives of science instruction (Edmonds 1982).

Disadvantages given for emphasising realism as a philosophy of education stress the fragmented knowledge that pupils may learn since each objective achieved emphasises parts of a whole. The teacher controls the science curriculum since he/she determines the objectives, learning opportunities, and evaluation procedures; pupils are not involved here in decision-making. The products of instruction in science are emphasised, leaving little room for process such as abstract thinking which is rather difficult to measure.

**Experimentalism in the Science Curriculum**

Experimentalists stress a problem-solving approach in the curriculum. They emphasise that individuals cannot know the real world as it truly is. Individuals, however, obtain experiences of this reality. With experiences, changes occur in one's thinking and believing. A changing world makes for problematic situations. Problems need identification and solutions sought. In the science curriculum, pupils with teacher guidance select a problem within an ongoing lesson or unit of study. The problem needs to be adequately delimited so that meaning and understanding is involved. An hypothesis is developed directly related to the stated problem. Information from a variety of sources is used by learners to arrive at a tentative solution. Experimentalists believe all knowledge to be tentative, not absolute.

The result might well involve changing and modifying the original hypotheses. The new hypothesis is then tried out in a concrete situation (Geiger, 1955). Problem solving may be used in all curriculum areas and in life itself. Knowledge here is used to solve problems and is not an end in and of itself. The practical and the utilitarian are emphasised within the framework of problem solving. Knowledge secured from a variety of sources has an application dimension. Knowledge then is useful to solve problems in a changing world, science included (Ediger 1995).

Experimentalists emphasise that school and society are one, not separate entities. Since groups in society select and solve problems, pupils in committees also need to be involved in cooperative learning stressing problem solving. School and society are one, not separate entities. Dewey (1915) is still very widely recognised as a leading advocate of experimentalism in teaching and learning. In integrating the learner with the self as well as with the social arena, he advocated four characteristics of pupils which have wide implications for the teaching of science. These are that pupils possess the social impulse in that they desire to work together with others in the curriculum; the constructive impulse in which learners like to learn by doing, not being passive individuals; the investigative and experimentalism inclination whereby pupils desire to learn by discovery rather than being told and lectured; and the creative or expressive impulse, rather than have rigid formal expectations for achievement.

Advantages given in emphasising experimentalism as a philosophy of teaching science are the following:

1. Pupil interest in science becomes paramount when they with teacher assistance identify problem areas. Interest in learning makes for effort in achieving.
2. Very young pupils in early primary grades may be involved in problem-solving experiences (Ediger 1994).
3. Problem solving is useful in all curriculum areas and in life itself when problems are selected and solutions sought.

Disadvantages of using experimentalism as a philosophy of education include problem selection being too difficult as well as problem-solving may not be a favourite style and way of learning for a few pupils. Also motivation may be lacking for some pupils to identify and solve problems.

## Idealism in the Science Curriculum

Idealist believe that one can receive ideas about the real world only. Thus one cannot know the real world as it truly is. Independent of the observer. Mental development in idealism becomes of utmost importance since an idea centred world is in evidence. Mind is real and needs development. As a leading idealist still quoted widely presently, Horne (1932) stressed the importance of the use of reason and rational thought in arriving at truth. Concepts and generalisations or universals such as justice, truth, goodness, ethics, and beauty have always existed and can be discovered by human beings. These universals are *a priori*, to an idealist, in that they have existed prior to human experience.

A subject centred curriculum in science is of paramount importance. In science lessons and units of study, pupils should achieve vital concepts, and generalisations. Depth teaching is needed to cultivate the intellect in guiding pupils achievement in science. A multimedia approach in learning is needed to assist pupils to achieve abstract ideas in science. The abstract to an idealist is superior to the concrete and semiconcrete in learning. The concrete and semiconcrete facets of learning in science are salient to the degree that learners attain the abstract such as vital facts, concepts, and generalisations in ongoing lessons and units of study. Since reading and writing, in particular, stress abstract learnings, they should not be minimised in the science curriculum.

To emphasise a subject centred curriculum as idealists recommend, an academically inclined teacher needs to teach in a scholarly way so that the objectives stressing intellectual goals are attained by pupils. Blanchard (1964) wrote:

The aim of thought from its very beginning, we saw, was at understanding. To understand anything meant to apprehend it in a system that rendered it necessary. The ideal of complete understanding would be achieved only when the system that rendered it necessary was not a system that itself was fragmentary and therefore contingent, but one that was all—inclusive and so organised internally that every part was linked to every other by intelligible necessity.

Advantages given for emphasising idealism as a philosophy of teaching science include the following:

1. Pupils are to achieve significant subject matter. Idealism emphasises the acquisition of vital content in science that pupils need to attain. Uses made of knowledge in science need to emphasise what is just to all, what is truthful, what is good in its application, what will truly stress ethical dimensions, and that which has beauty in its aesthetical areas.
2. Many pupils may be motivated to learn when an academic approach to learn science is stressed. This

might be especially appealing to the gifted and talented learners in science. All pupils need motivation to achieve and learn in science.

3. The abstract in idealism is preferred to the concrete and semiconcrete; relevant concepts, and generalisations, and other universals emphasise abstract goals in science teaching. Idealist advocate wholeness in knowledge, not fragmentation. Knowledge is related in all of its manifestations.

Disadvantages given for idealism as a philosophy in teaching and learning include minimising a hands on approach in learning science since the focal point of teaching is to have pupils develop well intellectually; placing emphasis upon universals much more so than specific—the latter is salient in pupils arriving at conclusions such as in science experiments; and integrating of knowledge to the point where science as a discipline is not as clearly defined as it might be. Idealists tend to stress that which goes beyond the five senses. Thus metaphysics and the *a priori* are salient to an idealist.

Quality sequence in science might be slighted when abstract phases of learning are more prized more highly than the concrete and semiconcrete. Most educators presently recommended a sequence of concrete, semiconcrete, to the abstract in teaching-learning situations. Quite similar in sequence. Bruner (1968) advocated using manipulative materials such as objects and items; followed by iconic materials such as audiovisual materials which are one step removed from the manipulative phase; and then symbolic activities which stresses the abstract including reading and writing.

## Existentialism and the Science Curriculum

Existentialists believe that one exists first and then finds his/her purposes in life; there are no standards to guide them being other than developed by the human race. Most existentialists advocate that people are condemned to be free with no *a priori* standards in life. Individuals then make or break themselves due to the kind of society wanted. Each person chooses and makes choices continually. To be human is to choose. If a person permits the self to have someone else makes one's own decisions, then the individual ceases to be human.

Combs (1972) stresses that the way individuals perceive a situation will assist in determining how the individual will behave. Perception is unique to the individual. Each person decides upon what is true, judges what is good, and decides upon plans of action. The science curriculum then must provide opportunities for pupils individually to decide what to learn, that is the objectives of instruction. The pupil needs to be heavily involved in selecting learning opportunities as well as methods of determining progress. The teacher is a guide and encourages pupil learning. The teacher, however, does not lecture nor determine the science curriculum for the individual pupil. A learning centres approach in teaching science may then be emphasised. Here, there are an adequate number of centres with quality tasks for learners at each centre. There needs to be more tasks than what a pupil can complete so that individual sequential choices may truly be made. A psychological, not logical, science curriculum is then in evidence. Each pupil may select tasks based on personal needs, interests, and purposes. The choice to be made is up to the individual pupils. If tasks do not meet personal needs of the involved learner, he/she might plan with the teacher what has merit and value to the pupil. A contract system might also be implemented in which the pupil with teacher guidance selects tasks to put into a contract for completion. The learner himself/herself is responsible for choices made. The individual perceives what is good and has quality. Knowledge is subjective, not objective to the existentialist. For example, in a values clarification session, the pupil determines what is moral in terms of uses made of science and technology; the teacher has a difficult position as a stimulator and of one who encourages pupil learning. Being humane in an absurd environment is a major goal for pupil achievement in existentialist thought and thinking.

## The Psychology of Education

Principles of learning from the psychology of learning give direction to the science in teaching-learning situations in ongoing lessons and units of study. Ediger (1994) lists the following criteria upon which educational psychologists agree should be followed by teachers:

1. Meaningful learning experiences should be provided pupils in the curriculum;
2. Interesting content and skills should be offered in lessons and units of study;
3. Purpose needs to be established within pupils for learning;
4. Quality sequence for pupil learning is a must;
5. Rational balance among knowledge, skills, and attitudinal objectives is important in the instructional arena.

**In Summary**

Science teachers need to select tenets from the philosophy of education which stress pupils attaining vital content, abilities, and attitudes. In reviewing the different philosophies of education discussed in this chapter, the following is salient from each philosophy:

1. Clarity in objectives of science instruction, carefully selected, as recommended by realists. However, it is important to avoid fragmenting knowledge obtained by pupils.
2. Problem-solving procedures as recommended by experimentalist. Life in society emphasises the importance of being able to solve personal and social problems.
3. Major concepts and generalisations, as universals in science, advocated by idealists.
4. Decision-making opportunities in science as recommended by existentialists. Each person needs to learn to make decisions.

I believe that a problem-solving philosophy encompasses the other three philosophies. I recommended problem solving as a major philosophy of education to emphasise in teaching science due to its relevance in the curriculum and in life itself. Problems abound and need solutions. Knowledge acquired then is instrumental or useful in problems to be solved which are selected by pupils with teacher guidance.

## REFERENCES

Blanshard, Brand (1964), *The Nature of Thought*, New York: Humanities Press, 492-517.

Bruner, Jerome (1968). *Toward A Theory of Instruction*, Cambridge, Massachusetts: Harvard University Press.

Combs, Arthur (1972), *Educational Objectives: Beyond Behavioural Objectives*, Washington, DC: Association for Supervision and Curriculum Development.

Dewey, John (1915), *School and Society*, Chicago: University of Chicago Press.

Ediger, Marlow (1995). *Demonstration Teaching in the Schools Education*, 114, 371-372.

Ediger, Marlow (1994). Mathematics, Problem Solving, and the Young Learner. *The Primary Teacher*, 19, 34-37.

Ediger, Marlow. Early Field Experiences in Teacher Education. *College Student Journal*, 28, 302-306.

Edmonds, Ron (1982). Programmes of School Improvement: An Overview. *Educational Leadership,* December, Volume 4.

Geiger, George W. (1955). An Experimentalist Approach to Education. *Modern Philosophies and Education*. Chicago, Illinois: National Society for the Study of Education, 54, 137-174.

Horne, Herman Harrell (1932). *The Democratic Philosophy of Education*. New York: The Macmillan Company, 325-340.

Mager, Robert F. (1972). *Goal Analysis*. Belmont, California: Fearon Publishers.

Skinner, B.F. (1979). *Beyond Freedom and Dignity*. New York: Alfred Knopf, Inc.

Tillman, Frank A., and others (1971). *Introductory Philosophy,* New York: Harper and Row, 550.

# Reading Achievement in Science

Reading in the curriculum area of science is vital, it is a way of identifying problems within the context of reading. Reading can also be an approach used to develop an hypothesis as well as test hypotheses. Reading is a skill that can complement a hands on approach in learning relevant facts, concepts, and generalisations pertaining to different units of study.

There are definite methods that science teachers should use to guide student reading in ongoing lessons of study.

## Guiding Science Reading

We have supervised student teachers in public schools for thirty years and have observed what appears to assist learners to achieve well when engaging in reading activities in science. These student teachers guided learners to be able to identify unknown words prior to their actual reading of subject matter in science. Possible new words to be encountered by students in reading science content were printed in neat manuscript letters on the chalk board. A few student teachers would print the possible unknown words within a sentence framework. In either case, the student teacher would observe pupils to see that they looked at each word being introduced carefully. Sometimes, the student teacher showed a picture or object directly related to the new word printed on the chalk board. Meaningful learning is very important. Thus, pupils should understand what is read and taught. This was in further evidence when the student teacher had pupils use the new words in sentences. If necessary, the student teacher would use the new word in a sentence that would harmonise with the content to be read in the science textbook(s).

Pupils tended to make minimal mistakes in word recognition when the student teacher introduced assumed unknown words to pupils prior to the actual reading of content. We believe strongly that pupils who do well in science tend to be good readers also. If pupils do not read as well as is necessary, they should be assisted by the science teacher to comprehend abstract symbols effectively so that meaningful learning takes place. Scientists in a laboratory setting do much reading since this is an important way of acquiring needed information. The teaching of science is not a reading course, but pupils need direction to identify needed words so that necessary subject matter can be found in a problem-solving situation. When words are introduced to pupils prior to the actual reading of content, learners sometimes make interesting discoveries such as words that are antonyms or synonyms. Vocabulary growth and development are important in reading science materials.

Prior to reading science content, the teacher should use pictures or other audio-visual materials to assist learners to secure background information. The necessary background information guides pupils to attach meaning to subject matter read. Pupils should not be word callers. They must understand what has been read. Using visuals or real objects that directly relate to the facts, concepts, and generalisations, read will help pupils to understand abstract words encountered. We find that learners very frequently identify problem areas when viewing the pictures which make the abstract comprehensible. These problem areas then provide reasons for reading. Reading is then done to secure answers/hypothesis to identified problems. Additional learning activities will be needed so that pupils develop reasonable hypotheses to problem areas. Experimentation should be the heart of the science curriculum with reading subject matter as another related avenue of learning.

After learners have completed the reading activity for the designated lesson, they may then pursue follow up experiences. Thus, pupils might use seminar methods to discuss in depth the subject matter read as well as the results of other learning activities. The seminar stresses depth, not survey learning.

Science teachers should always notice the kinds of errors pupils make in reading. Diagnosis is then in evidence. The following kinds of pupil errors in reading science content should be evaluated by the teacher:

1. Mistakes made in sound/symbol relationships in reading. The science teacher might then provide pupils with help in phonics as it is needed to understand content read;
2. Weaknesses noticed in pupils not being able to divide words into syllables so that each word is identified in a meaningful manner. There are common prefixes and suffixes which pupils may learn to recognise that have much transfer value from one situation to the next, e.g. "un" for a prefix and "ful" for a suffix. Once a word has been divided into meaningful parts, a pupil may almost immediately identify the unknown due to knowing the pronunciation of selected parts, e.g. not being able to identify the word "uneasy". However, when the pupil divides "uneasy" into component parts, he/she recognises "un" and "easy." The two syllables are then blended to pronounce correctly the word "uneasy";
3. Difficulties in using context clues. If a pupil does not recognise a word when reading science content, the teacher should ask learners to provide a word that fits in with the other words in the sentence. Too frequently, pupils provide a guess that is ridiculous for the unknown word. Certainly, pupils should provide a word that makes sense in relationship to the surrounding words in the sentences.

## Higher Levels of Cognition

Pupils should reflect upon subject matter encountered. To reflect requires thought. Thus pupils should think critically pertaining to ideas gleaned. When pupils think critically, they separate fact from opinion, fantasy from reality, and the relevant form the irrelevant. Learners may also detect content errors while reading. Pupils then must reflect upon the subject matter read so that understanding and concentration are in evidence. Also, learners will retain content longer if reflection upon ideas obtained is emphasised. A good science teacher realises that pupils need to become good readers since reading is one avenue of learning, among others.

Higher levels of cognition also require that pupils think creatively pertaining to ideas obtained. With, creative thinking, pupils secure originality of ideas. Uniqueness and novelty of response are salient in the creative thinking domain.

Problem-solving procedures as skills are vital for all pupils to develop. To solve problems, pupils need to be curious individuals who have a desire to learn. Reading is one way to obtain necessary information to solve problems. Thus to solve problems, pupils need to identify a problem area, develop an hypothesis, test the hypothesis, and revise the hypothesis if needed. In each step of problem solving, learners may read from the science textbook or/and tradebooks, e.g. pupils might identify one or more problems in science through reading. Generally, additional learning activities will be in the offing so that pupils may select and solve problems in depth rather than use survey approaches.

## In Conclusion

A quality programme of reading in science stresses learners acquiring vital facts, concepts, and generalisations in ongoing lessons and units of study. Reading, along with other activities and experiences, should provide a variety of endeavours to secure pupil interest. Various endeavours also guide the science teacher in providing for individual differences in the classroom so that each pupil might learn as much as possible.

Reading in science needs to emphasise higher levels of cognition. Thus pupils develop skills in critical and creative thinking as well as in problem solving. Learners need to achieve

**optimally in science. The world of science surrounds everyone and has made for inventions and technology that truly are outstanding and revered.**

19

# Building Background Knowledge for Student Reading

A major reason for a lack of comprehension is that students do not assess the prerequisites for reading a given selection. The literacy teacher has an important responsibility in assisting learners to attain the necessary background information which is directly related to the ensuing reading activity. Objectives here must be carefully chosen so that increased effectiveness in student comprehension is in evidence. Which plans of reading instruction may be used to guide students in achieving the necessary background content?

## Teaching to Develop Increased Comprehension

What might assist in developing student readiness for meaningful reading of content? There are several valid procedures. Advance organisers may be used in reading instruction. Here, the teacher explains main ideas to students which will appear in ensuing print. These main ideas relate to salient ideas to be read by students. Relevant supporting facts might help to clarify main ideas. Clarity of presentation by the teacher is vital. He/she may assess the self by noticing how effectively learners comprehend subject matter in reading. Feedback to the teacher provides knowledge of future revisions which may need to be made in using the advanced organisers' approach. Certainly with quality main ideas in their repertoire, students should increased comprehension of subject matter read.

A second procedure might well be to assist students to view the illustrations embedded in the print script. Each salient illustration should be discussed with learners prior to the oral/ silent reading activity. Students may then predict what the subject matter to be read will contain. Each prediction might well be checked with comprehended ideas. This approach could be integrated with the advanced organiser concept previously discussed. There is room also to have students notice carefully the new words to be encountered. These may be printed in neat, manuscript letters prior to student reading of the subject matter. Students need to take careful note of each word and use it in context so that meaning is established to assist in reading comprehension. The teacher may then assess how well students correctly recall the previously presented words when engaged in the ongoing reading experience. Feedback to the teacher always provides information on future ways of increasing teaching effectiveness.

A third approach in providing background information to students is to look at context pictures in the materials to be read and then make predictions of what the ensuing script will emphasise. So far, this sounds familiar from the previously mentioned procedures in having students build readiness to comprehend what will be read. This is carried one step further by having the teacher read aloud the content as students follow along in their reader. It is best if a large book is used for all to see clearly, as the small group proceeds in observing the words as the teacher reads aloud, followed by students also joining in for the second read aloud. Rereading may be done as often as is needed. Observation of students to notice if they are following the script carefully is salient since learners will then be expected to read on their very own. By this time, the background information is there for meaningful reading by students individually. Students may also check their predictions after initially having viewed the illustrations before the read aloud.

The big book differs from other procedures in that these young students:

1. read the entire selection together with teacher guidance in order that there may be success for sequential, individual progress in possessing background information;
2. experience holism to identify words in context and comprehend ideas through assistance from the teacher read aloud;
3. may avoid pitfalls in reading readiness when using the teacher read aloud model to comprehend subject matter.

A fourth approach in assisting students to receive background information prior to reading a given selection is to use a variety of audio visual aids to clarify meanings. University student teachers whom we supervised in the schools used a diverse materials of instruction. One student teacher together with the cooperating teacher showed overlays and the overhead projector to show land ownership and farming methods during the later Middle Ages in a social studies unit of study by that title. Thus, one-third of the tillable land on a manor was cultivated for fall seeding in a given calendar year; one third was left fallow, while another third part was seeded in spring. Beyond the three field system for tillable land, a separate set of overlays indicated the woodlands, pasture land for cattle, as well as the layout of the medieval castle, the present huts, the church, the mill, and storage facilities for agricultural crops. The overlays were clear and colourful. Students were extremely attentive and contributed much in a related discussion to indicate understanding of background ideas.

Another university student teacher showed a brief video tape on the walled city of Jerusalem to develop background information within students to attach meaning to the Crusades in a unit on the Middle East. She pointed out the fortified walled city with its eight entrances leading into Jerusalem. The Church of the Holy Sepulcher was noted as an important place wanted by the Crusaders since it contained what they believed to be the Tomb of Christ. This video provided needed information for students to understand the Crusaders and the Crusades when reading on this topic from the basal text. The video contents amplified information on the importance then and now of the walled city of Jerusalem. We do believe students benefited much from the necessary information to understand the new subject matter to be read. The student teacher did not call attention to the new words prior to students reading the assignment silently. Instead, she pronounced unknown words, immediately, as students indicated a need for word recognition assistance. Quality comprehension was revealed during the discussion which followed.

A third student teacher used the illustrations in the next to provide learner background information in order to attach meaning to subject matter to be read. Instead of calling attention to new words printed on the chalkboard for mastery prior to student silent reading of the content, she had students survey the basal text lesson to identify new words in context. These were printed on the chalkboard in neat manuscript letters. The student teacher pointed to each as they were being rehearsed orally for correct identification. This method of building background information with text illustrations and students identifying new words, learners were truly involved in achieving. Active participants in learning rather than passive individuals was in evidence.

We would like to mention one additional experience for students which assisted in building background information for reading. Here, a hands on approach was used. In a small, rural city, students planted seeds in containers prior to reading about seeding crops, in a unit on farming. Each student brought a small metal can with soil for seeding the wheat. The teacher had a few extra containers for those who did not bring one. The learning by doing attempted to simulate seeding of grain. Generally, there is excitement when students are involved in manual dexterity activities.

Reading teachers must try out new ideas to determine ways of providing background information within students prior to their reading print materials. There are several issues involved here:

1. Should all students experience a special method of providing background information such as discussing the illustrations in the text. We observed a gifted sixth grade class being taught in which the teacher did not discuss the pictures therein, prior to student reading. Instead, she told of personal experiences in going fishing whereby students would then read on the same topic. Students injected their own fishing experiences in the discussion. They were then asked to read the selection on the author's fishing experiences. The lesson went along very well since these gifted individuals seemingly had considerable preceding information on fishing. This was revealed in the pre/post reading discussions.
2. Is an excessive amount of time spent on introducing "new words" when it is quite obvious students in class are, in some cases, highly familiar with these words? The same question might be raised about background experiences for learners in that students do acquire much information from the media and discussions in the home setting. However, the teacher always needs to be aware of gaps existing in knowledge possessed by learners;
3. Is the reading curriculum too teacher centred? To be sure, there needs to be adequate teacher direction and guidance in teaching and learning situations. However, it is good to assist students to become independent readers. There needs to be rational balance between teacher determination and student input into the reading curriculum.

## Additional Methods of Assisting Students to Achieve Information

There are informal, indirect means of assisting students to achieve background information. All schools should emphasise Drop Everything and Read (DEAR) programmes. In this way, each student may choose what to read independently. Generally, a student will select a library book for reading based on personal interest. The interest factor brings to bear subject matter knowledge possessed by the learner. In this way, the student who chooses the book for reading brings his/her own background information in understanding the ensuing subject matter. With sequential library books chosen for reading, the student is the chooser of which possessed subject matter becomes relevant to the reading situation.

Second, when the controlled reader was emphasised as late as the 1970s, there were degrees of repetition in wording and in subject matter read. There still are elements of controlling the new words emphasised and subject matter content stressed. To have no control would be highly frustrating for elementary age students in particular. However, there needs to be adequate newness of words and ideas expressed in print to stimulate student achievement in reading. The controlling of vocabulary terms as well as subject matter content makes it possible to have developmentally appropriate content for students.

Third, programmed reading has built in background information inside their programmes, be it in textbook or computerised form. A student, however, must be ready to read a programme so that he/she may respond to each item to be learned. From one programmed step to the next, close sequencing is involved. In quality programmes then, a student, in most cases, will respond correctly ninety-five per cent of the times. A student, for example, then reads several sentences, responds to a multiple choice item covering content read. He/she does not read several paragraphs or pages before responding to a multiple choice test item to assess comprehension. Rather, a shorter amount is read before being assessed on the correctness of the response given. If a student responded correctly with the answer given by the programmer, he/she is rewarded. If an incorrect response was given, the student then sees the correct response as given by the programmer and is also ready for the next programmed item. Basically, the same order is followed by students with read, respond, and then check the student given answer. Each item to be read in the

**programme provides *background information* for the next few ideas to be read. To make certain a student is on the right track continuously, the answer given to the few sentences read, is assessed to insure correctness.**

## In Closing

**Each student needs background information to understand the subject matter to be read. Different procedures of reading instruction vary in how the information is to be secured. Having adequate background information is necessary so that a student comprehends and attaches meaning to subject matter read.**

## REFERENCES

Dewey, John (1916), *Democracy and Education*. New York: The Macmillan Company.

Ediger, Marlow (1995), *Philosophy and Curriculum Development*, Kirksville, Missouri: Simpson Publishing Company, 27-28.

Ediger, Marlow, and D. Bhaskara Rao (2000), "Philosophical Considerations in Teaching Mathematics." *Teaching Mathematics Successfully*. New Delhi, India: Discovery Publishing House, Chapter Two.

Ediger, Marlow (2000), *Teaching Reading Successfully*. New Delhi, India: Discovery Publishing House, Chapter Six.

Ediger, Marlow (2001), "Social Studies Children's Literature," *Teaching Social Studies Successfully*. New Delhi, India: Discovery Publishing House, Chapter Eight.

Ediger, Marlow (2000), "Phonics and Poetry in the Curriculum," *Experiments in Education*, 28 (8), 131-135.

Ediger, Marlow (2001), Evaluation of Pupil Achievement in Science," *Teaching Science Successfully*. New Delhi, India: Discovery Publishing House, Chapter Sixteen.

Ediger, Marlow (1995), "Why Seminar Methods in Literature?" *Arizona English Bulletin*, 37 (2), 59-60.

*Education Week* (April 18, 2001), "*A Quiet Crisis:* Unprepared for High Stakes," p. 1.

Goleman, Daniel (1995), *Emotional Intelligence*. New York: Bantam Books.

O' Neill, William F. (1981), *Educational Ideologies*. Santa Monica, California: Goodyear Publishing Company, p. 168.

# Theories of Learning and the Reading Teacher

**Theories of learning may be difficult for teachers to understand and implement. Schools of education at universities must be certain that prospective teachers are highly knowledgeable about relevant theories of learning and become skillful in their implementation. These theories provide direction and guidance in developing teaching units, lesson plans, as well as teaching strategies. A prospective teacher should not flounder nor group haphazardly when planning and using diverse teaching strategies.**

## Understanding and Applying Theories of Learning

Behaviourism is presently emphasised much by educators in the curriculum arena. A behaviourist believes strongly in specifying objectives for student attainment prior to instruction. Each objective written must be highly specific so that a teacher can measure learner achievement after instruction. Ideally, there should be no leeway for interpretation as to the meaning of any one objective. Other teachers viewing the written objective(s) would agree as to what will be learned by students as a result of teaching.

Behaviourist advocate that learning opportunities are to be aligned with their respective objectives. Each opportunity for learning then guides students to achieve the stated objectives. Tests to measure student achievement are also aligned with the objectives. Results from students taking the tests should then be valid in that what was tested harmonised with the stated objectives. With clearly written test items, reliability should be in evidence since students staking the tests should receive comparable or consistent results, be it with test retest, split-half, and/or alternative forms reliability. Objectivity in test results is a key concept stressed by behaviourist. Numerical results are in the offing such as per cent of items answered correctly by the student, percentile rank, quartile deviation, and/or standard deviation.

Most behaviourist recommend operant conditioning procedures be used in teaching-learning situations. With operant conditioning, teachers reward correct responses given by learners. This strengthens the connections between the stimulus (S) with the response (R). Reinforcement theory then emphasises rewarding correct responses given by learners in the classroom. The rewards can be immediate such as with verbal praise or with physical prizes given by the teacher to students who respond correctly in ongoing lessons and units of study. Verbal praise is relatively easy to administer whereas with physical prizes, the teacher must communicate clearly to learners what they are to attain to receive a prize. A ratio procedure may be used. Thus for every ten correct responses, a physical prize is given. Ratios may be fixed or variable. If the prize is difficult to give upon a student responding correctly in a ratio situation, a token economy may be implemented. Thus instead of the prize being given when due, a token can be given which may be exchanged for a prize at a more suitable time such as on Friday afternoon. Fixed and varied intervals of time may be used also as a basis for rewarding students. Here, learners again must know what to do to secure a prize during a time interval such as five minutes of not disrupting the class. It is better if higher standards than the five minutes can be emphasised, but one must begin at a feasible entry point. As soon as possible, the interval of time should be longer in duration than the five minutes of not disturbing other learners in the classroom. In cases such as these, the term "behaviour modification" is used. The concepts of "successive approximations" and "shaping" become important. With rewards being given continuously for good behaviour in doing well in school, the successive approximations in rewarding assist learners to achieve the ultimate or target behaviour. The target behaviour is the kind of person the teacher desires the student to become. Shaping of behaviour in a desired direction through reinforcement guides, hopefully, in students becoming effective learners

Teachers through faculty meetings and staff development programmes can learn to implement tenets of behaviourism and reinforcement theory. The writer assisted his student teachers (STs) to write objectives in measurable terms for pupils to achieve. The ST announced to pupils what they are to learn as a result of instruction. After teaching and learning has occurred, the student teacher measured if pupils had attained the predetermined objectives. A different teaching strategy was used for pupils who had not achieved the stated objectives. With few pupils in the class, eleven in number plus the assistance of the cooperating teacher (CT), it was relatively easy to shape learner behaviour. For example, pupils were working an exercise in their workbooks and for each sentences that was corrected therein, a stamp having the image of a turkey was stamped next to the corrected sentence. Each sentence originally was written incorrectly and pupils were to make desired corrections. With a 5.5 pupils to teacher ratio here, the ST and CT managed a reward system quite well. The rewards were continuous to shape learner behaviour through successive approximations.

Toward the other end of the continuum the Gestalt theory of learning stresses wholes rather than parts or specifics in the curriculum. Gestaltists have always believed that the whole is greater than the sum of the parts. There are numerous programmes of instruction that emphasise Gestalt theory of learning. Individualised reading advocates pupils reading the entire self-selected trade book before having a conference with the teacher. Parts such as phonetic analysis and syllabication skills taught to pupils in many programmes of reading instruction are not emphasised in individualised reading as a separate facet of teaching. Rather, during the conference, the teacher may stress phonics/syllabication as it is needed with the individual pupil. Thus in orally reading a selection to the teacher, the pupil may reveal he/she needs assistance in a few reading skills. A Gastalt psychology of learning is then in evidence since the pupil reads entire library/trade books before having a conference with the teacher. Interest gleaned from reading ideas propels the pupil to improve in fluency in the reading curriculum. Another procedure of teaching that stressed wholeness or Gestalt is whole language approaches in writing. The whole of writing is more than grammar, usages, spelling, indentation, and sequence of content, paragraphs, and legible handwriting. Ideas are expressed in whole language approaches in writing. The mechanics of writing aid in the full expression of ideas, content, facts, concepts and generalisations. An ST supervised by the writer revealed her strong beliefs in Gastalt theory in word and deed by guiding pupils to:

1. read entire self-selected library books directly related to an ongoing social studies unit. Ideas secured from reading were brought into the discussion of unit content as the need arose. There was no analysis of word attack skills involving the pupil who read the book. The pupil chose what to share with other learners as the discussion progressed in the ongoing unit of study;
2. write business letters to order free and inexpensive materials to obtain charts and pictures for the ongoing social studied unit. Pupils individually wrote the entire business letter before selected mechanics of writing were analysed. From the whole to the part(s) was being emphasised here.

## Stimulus—Response Versus Gestalt Theory of Learning

Presently, there is considerable disagreement as to which theory of learning should receive mast emphasis. Below are listed additional programmes of instruction that stress S-R theory of learning:

1. State mandated objectives for pupils to achieve. The objectives are generally written in measurable terms;

2. Individually prescribed instruction which has predetermined objectives for student attainment. Based on the stated objectives, learners are given a pretest to determine art which specific point or objective a student should begin;
3. Mastery learning which emphasises specific objectives for student achievement. Either a student has or has not attained an objective as a result of instruction.

Additional programmes of teaching stressing Gastalt theory of learning include the following:

1. *A literature based reading curriculum.* Major stress here is placed upon quality literature being read by learners rather than a strong sequential phonics/ syllabication emphasis in reading. The latter emphasises dividing the reading curriculum into small segments of learning for pupils to acquire;
2. Basal reading programmes can be quite holistic if the teacher emphasises learners achieve ideas rather than highly precise skills such as word analysis;
3. *Experiences charts developed by pupils with teacher guidance.* The content for the experience chart comes from pupils based on an experience they have had such as an excursion right on the school grounds. Learners then provide the ideas from the experience to the teacher who records these statements on the chalkboard. Pupils may then see talk written down. The experience chart concept stresses the wholeness of the experience of pupils and this is printed so it can be read by young pupils as the teacher points to words and phrases. Emphasis is placed upon the pupils reading the ideas they provided for the experience chart.

## In Closing

Theories of learning provide direction and guidance to the teacher when making curricular decisions. It is quite obvious that a teacher leaning toward behaviourism and stimulus response psychology of learning would teach differently from one who stresses Gestalt psychology.

Teachers must understand the diverse tenets in each psychology of learning. Each school of thought may then be implemented in actual teaching-learning situations. Whichever psychology is chosen must assist the learner and pupil to achieve optimally.

# 21

# Tips in Reading Instruction

There are definite tips I would like to recommend in the teaching of reading which might well assist pupils to achieve more optimally. I have gleaned these tips from supervising student teachers and regular teachers in the public schools over a thirty year period of time. The purpose of writing this manuscript is to provide reading teachers with information which, hopefully, will assist to achieve more optimally.

Tip number one. Too frequently phonics is taught to the class as a whole on the primary grade levels. Thus, each pupil in the class receives the same/similar amount of instruction in phonics. Within a class there are pupils who are quite proficient in using phonics to read well. At the same time there are pupils who could benefit much from phonics teaching to unlock unknown words. I recommend that phonics instruction be individualised whereby a learner secures help in unlocking new words as needed. A pupil then may need very little or perhaps no assistance in phonics instruction. Whereas, others need a considerable amount of help in associating symbols with sounds to identify unknown words.

If phonics is taught prior to its use, pupils tend to forget these abstract learnings before application is needed to identify the unknown word. It appears that the time to teach phonics is when it is needed by a pupil in a contextual situation, not in isolation from the act of reading a given selection. There should be as little interruption in the process of reading subject matter when assisting a learner in phonics. Reading involves sequence, phrasing, meaning, and comprehension. Learning phonics for the sake of doing so has little or no value. However, phonics is valuable when it guides pupils to become independent readers who understand content read.

Tip Number Two. There are pupils who need help to read in thought units. Thus proper phrasing is needed in the act of reading to further comprehension. We have noticed pupils who read a sentence incorrectly in the following manner: The boy with/the red/bicycle rods away rapidly. It almost sounds as if "the bicycle rode away rapidly." These pupils can identify each word basically, in reading, but fail to read content in a meaningful manner due to poor phrasing.

We recommend here that the teacher or a capable reader/ aid cover up words so that the content has to be read in proper thought units such as "The boy with the red bicycle/rode away rapidly." Thus, "rode away quickly" would need covering until "The boy with the red bicycle" has been read in a meaningful thought unit. It is best if the teacher has the time to provide this assistance. The goal for pupils to achieve when reading in proper thought units is to read fluently and comprehend has been read.

Tip Number Three. Too frequently teachers want to pronounce unknown words to pupils before the learner has a chance to analyse that word. It is only good to have pupils become independent in recognising words. The sooner pupils can become self sufficient in word identification the better. Life itself emphasises that each person depend upon the self as much as possible.

Reading teachers then need to have pupils determine the pronunciation and identification of unknown words. A reasonable amount of time needs to be given here, perhaps five seconds before pronouncing an unknown word to a pupil. Even then it is best to provide ways of unlocking unknown words to the pupil, such as having the learner notice the beginning or ending letter. These letters then need to be associated with related sounds in a grapheme/phoneme relationship.

Tip Number Four. We find that teachers should assist pupils to use contextual clues more so than is commonly done. This is a good method of pupils determining not only an unknown word but also the meaning of a word. A word that a pupil places into a sentence that appears to be unknown must make sense in relationship to the other words in the sentence being read. If pupils then use context approaches in ascertaining an unknown word as well as its meaning, the chances are that success in reading might well be in service much more so as compared to not using context clues. Meaningful reading is in evidence if context clues are used by learners when reading. Why? The word supplied by a learner for an unknown word must make sense when context clues are being emphasised.

Tip Number Five. Teachers need to help pupils think about what has been read. In this way, pupils are using knowledge in new situations. The *why* and *how* questions are good to stress when emphasising higher levels of pupil cognition. The following are examples of *why* questions:

1. Why do you think that way? This question pertains to a comment made by a learner in order to seek a rationale for a statement;
2. Why do you feel Mr. Wheeler had worked hard at his job?
3. Why do you believe things seemed to turn out bad for Willie?

*How* kinds of questions stress the following:

1. How did yesterday's story end differently as compared to today's story?
2. How do the two main characters differ and how are they alike in comparing today's with yesterday's story?

Pupils should be guided to think critically, creatively, and engage in problem solving in the reading curriculum. These levels of cognition take time to develop within pupils; in fact, they are ongoing in development throughout an individual's life time.

Tip Number Six. Teachers need to work at securing pupil's attention at the beginning as well as throughout the reading lesson. We find that teachers too frequently do not have a strategy to interest and motivate pupils in reading. Reading instruction then becomes routine and boring to pupils. We would suggest the following:

1. Initiate a lesson using a new approach such as showing a related videotape, a set of illustrations, selected objects, puppets and marionettes, and drawings, among others. Relate these materials of instruction to the content in the story. Change off by using the activities as developmental or culminating experiences for pupils that relate story content;
2. Use voice inflection properly and a stimulating voice to obtain and maintain learner attention throughout the reading lesson. Teacher enthusiasm does tend to reflect within pupils. The focal point in teaching pupils is to guide optimal achievement in reading;
3. Introduce for pupils to see, trade books that relate to the story being read and discussed. I frequently reflect upon what motivated me in reading in the elementary school years. The answer is I really enjoyed reading the trade books in our rural school library. Teachers here frequently brought in additional books for pupils to read from the public library. Encourage pupils to tell during reading class what they read from other sources and materials at home or during free reading time in school;
4. Vary approaches used in teaching reading with the use of pantomime, creative dramatics, and formal dramatics to breathe life into content studied in reading. Pupils reveal what has been learned by dramatizing content read. There are many ways to vary teaching methods and strategies in the teaching of reading;
5. Encourage pupil achievement in reading, do not discourage. Always, reward what is positive about a pupil's achievement in reading.

Tip Number Seven. Answer parent's questions about the reading programme by responding in a positive manner. There may be questions pertaining to the following:

1. How much of the basics is being stressed in reading?
2. If enough phonics is being taught?
3. Why the parents child is not doing better in reading?
4. What can be done in the home setting to help the pupil do better in reading?
5. Might more difficult reading materials help a child achieve more rapidly in reading?

Each teacher needs to discuss openly and freely questions raised by parents about how their child is taught in reading. Together the teacher and parents can work cooperatively in developing the best reading programme possible for a child. We believe parents can help pupils much in the home setting so that improved reading on the pupil's part is in evidence.

Tip Number Eight. Praise each pupil for achieving in reading. The sincere praise should be given to all in a classroom Thus regardless of ability and achievement levels, each pupil may be rewarded in moving from where he/she is presently in reading achievement to a higher level of accomplishment. The gains for selected learners in reading accomplishment may be small for a specific period of time; however, even with small gains in achievement a pupils needs to be recognised for achievement in reading. Hopefully, this will spur pupils on to greater progress in reading. The reading teacher needs to provide for individual differences so that each pupil may achieve as much as possible.

Basically, we are opposed to offering physical prizes to pupils as rewards for doing well in reading. Instead we have found that pupils do better in reading achievement in sincere verbal praise is used.

Tip Number Nine. Meeting esteem and belonging needs of pupils is important. The reading teacher needs to find out what hobbies, talents, and interests pupils individually possess.

These strengths need to recognising and brought in to the reading curriculum. The teacher needs to make use of unique abilities of pupils by integrating these in to ongoing lessons and units of study in reading. Each pupil desires to be recognised for hobbies, talents, and interests possessed. A good self concept is important for pupils to have. Reading achievement should then increase on the part of each learner if wholesome self concepts are in evidence. We have found that teachers who recognise pupil's diverse abilities assist learners to be more highly motivated in the school curriculum. Pupils also need to feel they belong and are wanted in a group setting. Educational literature stresses much that pupils work in cooperative learning endeavours. The reading teacher must study learners and place pupils into groups that are accepting. Learners need feel they belong. Feelings of belonging are important for pupils. A classroom and school setting houses pupils and no one desires to be an isolate and shunned by others. Cooperative learning can assist pupils to achieve more optimally if members are chosen carefully for each group.

Tip Number Ten. The school needs to meet as many physiological needs of pupils as possible. Nutritious breakfasts should be served to all pupils desiring to participate. Hopefully, quality hot lunches with proper nutrition are served in all schools. A hungry pupil cannot do well in reading.

Pupils who are tired may achieve very poorly in learning to read. In parent/teacher conferences, emphasis should be placed upon pupils having sleep and rest needs met. A conscientious parent will want to have personal needs of offspring met so that more optimal achievement in reading is possible.

The above named ten tips in teaching reading are important in assisting pupils to achieve as well as possible. We would suggest using different creative approaches by reading teachers to guide pupils to remedy deficiencies. We have suggested a few approaches, but there are others. We would also suggest that for young children, in particular, schools implement tenets of Reading Recovery programmes is instruction. Here, for thirty minutes a day, a first grade pupils receives thirty minutes of one on one instruction, uninterrupted in reading. There is little time then for things that interfere with a pupil receiving continuous teaching with a single teacher in reading. Tenets of Reading Recovery should be used with older pupils; time limits could be flexible here. A second approach that we recommend is to have tape recordings that go along directly with a library book or textbook in reading. The learner then may follow along with the taped voice as he/she views words contained in abstract print. This procedure helps pupils much in word recognition and reading more challenging materials than would otherwise be the case. The cassette recording then identifies words for pupils in reading.

A third procedure we recommend to help pupils in reading is to have pupils select and read sequentially their very own books from the classroom or centralised library. Perhaps, books can be borrowed too from the public library for pupils to read. After reading a library book, the pupil may have a conference with the teacher to evaluate comprehension of content as well as word recognition approaches when the learner reads orally to the teacher in the conference. The teacher can then briefly record that which the pupil needs more assistance in as far as reading achievement is concerned. A fourth procedure in teaching reading is to use personalised procedures. Thus with an experience, inside or outside the classroom, the teacher may lead pupils to provide content for a chart. Directly related to the experience, learners present the ideas and the teacher records the content on the chalkboard or computer. After the chart has been completed, the teacher guides learners to read the content by pointing to words and phrases, on the chalkboard or on the monitor. Experiences of the learner provide the content for the chart; readiness has then been provided for the act of reading. Each chart can be filed for future reading by pupils.

## The Psychology of Teaching Reading

We believe strongly that there are definite principles from the psychology of learning that should be used in reading instruction. These principles of learning from educational psychology are the following:

1. Make teaching and learning procedures as interesting as possible for learners. With pupil interest, increased proficiency in reading should be an end result;
2. Establish purpose for pupils to participate in ongoing lessons and units of study. Reasons are then in evidence to learners as to why it is important to learn and achieve;
3. Provide for individual differences among pupils in reading instruction. Pupils differ from each other in many ways including achievement in reading. Should the teacher not respect these differences by having pupils read materials at and of different levels of complexity? Each pupil needs to be respected and assisted to achieve as well as possible in reading;
4. Give continuous opportunities for pupils to experience success in learning. This is positive to do so. Successful learners in reading achieve more optimally than those facing failure excessively;
5. Assist pupils to attach meaning to what is being learned. If pupils understand that which is being learned, they will retain content and skills longer. Achievement in reading is sequential and needs careful planning by the reading teacher. Pupils also need to be involved in determining sequence such as individualised reading whereby the learner chooses sequentially library books to read;
6. Show enthusiasm for teaching. Teacher enthusiasm for teaching reading does reflect within pupils when the latter is learning to read at increasing levels of complexity;
7. Share with pupils what you are reading. Bring the content down to the understanding level of pupils. We believe that even Plato's Republic can be told to pupils in a manner whereby pupils attach meaning to the content;

8. Use sustained silent reading to show that you the teacher also like to read. The entire class together with the teacher are reading during the time devoted to sustained silent reading. The reading teacher is a model then for pupils in the classroom;
9. Read orally to pupils during story time so that pupils can enjoy quality literature in a relaxed manner. Look at pupils as the reading is being done. For young children, it is good to show the related illustrations in the library book as you read orally to them;
10. Indicate your interest in the welfare of each pupil. This is more necessary than ever before when many children come from single parent homes and/or divorce appears to be minimising the stability of family life. Be aware of possible child abuse of individual pupils. Pupils are young and vulnerable due to their age and lack of experience. The teacher can definitely be a stabilising force here.

## In Closing

The reading teacher needs to guide each pupil to achieve as well as possible in reading, the child's future requires the ability to read well and comprehend thoroughly what has been read. Word attack skills must be taught to pupils as needed. These word attack skills include:

1. phonics and syllabication;
2. context clues and meaning of content read;
3. pictorial clues and configuration clues.

Reading for meaning and comprehension are major goals in reading. Thus pupils need to read to achieve higher cognitive objectives such as reading to:

1. think critically and creatively;
2. solve identify and problems;
3. secure facts, concepts, and main ideas;
4. apply what has been read;
5. detect bias and overgeneralising.

Pupils need acceptance of each teacher so that feelings of belonging are in evidence. Learners need recognition for talents possessed in order that esteem needs may be met. All schools should assist pupils to have psychological needs met through nutritious food at breakfast time and during the noon meal. Cooperation with agencies in the community might well provide needy pupils with eye glasses and hearing aids, as well as other needs that a low income level home cannot meet.

The whole child needs to be observed to determine needs that a pupil has. Each need should be remedied as soon as possible. Teachers, administrators, and school counselors should view pupils holistically and make provision for optimal development of each learner. The pupils needs to achieve optimally presently in reading and other curriculum areas so that he/she will have an excellent chance of being ready for the workplace as an adult and achieve as well as possible. Being able to read well is important in the world of work. It is also importance as a leisure time activity. Each reading teacher needs to take his/her professional responsibility with utmost sincerity. Hopefully, an end result will be a nation of readers who do well in endeavours involving reading.

# Grouping Students in Reading

There are numerous means in grouping learners for instruction in reading. Teachers are supervisors need to study and analyse diverse plans. Adopted grouping procedures need to guide students to achieve optimally. Which approaches in placing learners into groups might be utilised to aid student progress in reading?

## Homogeneous Grouping

Many teachers group students homogeneously to minimise a wide range of reading achievement. Thus, a more uniform set of learners in demonstrating skills in reading is in evidence. Perfect uniformity will never be in evidence. It is easier to provide for individual levels in reading achievement if the range of achievement is somewhat uniform. Within a classroom, the teacher might then place the top, middle, and slower achievers into three different reading groups. A single series of basal readers may be utilised in teaching and learning. Or, multiple series might also be used in ongoing lessons and units. A major goal of reading instruction is to guide each student, whether in the fast, average, or slower group, to learn as much as possible.

Ediger wrote:

Teachers may find it easier to teach a given group of learners if homogeneous grouping is in evidence as compared to heterogeneous grouping since the range of achievement will not be as great within a class. However, teachers may not like to teach a class of slow learners as well as those who achieve at a faster rate of speed. The attitude of the teacher, of course, may be reflected with learners. Since the range of achievement in a class may be very great in heterogeneous grouping, it may pose a problem for some teachers in providing for individual differences. In certain methods of teaching it may not matter much if heterogeneous or homogeneous grouping is utilised. For example, in individualised reading, each pupil basically selects his own library book to read. He generally selects a book which is on his reading level. His own reading of the library book will involve a pace which should be in harmony with being able to comprehend the contents adequately. Each pupil in a class will read at a different rate of speed. Also, each learner will select a library book which differs in complexity from other library books selected for reading by other children in the classroom. Thus, individual differences can be provided for regardless of capacity and achievement levels of pupils in a class or group.

Advocates of the nongraded school emphasise students being grouped homogeneously based on reading achievement. Thus, teachers need to identify reading progress of students, as early as possible, perhaps in grade one. The top achievers are taught in one room, the next best achievers in the second room, and placing the slowest learners in reading in a separate room.

Adjustments, no doubt, will need to be made if a learner progresses more rapidly or slowly in reading compared to previous times. He/she may then need to be placed in a different room so that increased homogeneity is in evidence. The teacher in a nongraded school will also have three reading groups within a room. The range of achievement within each group is then further minimised. Flexible grouping needs to be emphasised for each student in reading. The involved learner needs to be placed in a classroom and group within a room whereby continuous progress can take place.

Dufay wrote:

It is a startling truth: No two snowflakes are alike! But this fact regarding snowflakes is of small consequence to the destiny of our nation. Our greater concern must be for facts relating to a more complex group, infinitely more precious and more crucial to the future welfare of our society—our children. Common sense, as well as experience and intuition, tells us that children are indeed also in the no-two-are-alike category.

Homogeneous grouping in reading instruction does not emphasise:

1. mixed achievement levels of students within a set of learners;
2. rigid means of grouping which remain stable in time and space.

## Individualised Reading

Individualised reading emphasises an open-ended curriculum. Thus, the learner may select sequentially which library books to read and to omit. An adequate number of book need to be available to learners to stimulate interest in reading. Also, the library books need to be on diverse levels of reading achievement. Thus, the slow, average, and talented reader may select a library book of personal interest on a level of complexity which meets personal aspirations.

After having selected and read a library book, the involved student then engages in a conference with the teacher to appraise reading achievement. The student and the teacher may appraise the following: interest in the library book, quality of comprehension of content read, and proficiency in oral reading. The teacher needs to record observations made, inherent in the conference.

Veatch wrote:

One of the advantages of individualised reading over other methods is the elimination of pressure and tension from the student in his attempt to meet the standards of his group. Why should he be compared with anyone else? He is not exactly like anyone else. When group competition is removed and the child is allowed to compete against himself, his own ability becomes the standard by which he is judged and tensions and pressures will give way to a more relaxed and more efficient type of study. The removal of this pressure should also eliminate the development of possible emotional blockages and undesirable attitudes toward reading.

Maximum efficiency in the use of a child's time is another advantage of individualised reading. The student does not drill with a group on words which only certain members in the group do not know. Instead, he spends time only on his own list of words *he* does not know. The amount of time which the student spends in silent reading is also increased because he need not wait while others are reading orally. Instead, he spends his time in doing his own silent reading or in activities related to this reading.

Individualised reading does not emphasise:

1. Teachers selecting regarding materials for students. Guidance is given only to those learners who are not able to pursue the reading of sequential library books;
2. Teachers solely selecting objectives, learning activities, and appraisal procedure;
3. A formal, structured reading curriculum in which scope and sequence has been determined for the learner;
4. The use of specific, measurable objectives;
5. Management systems of instruction with sequential learnings determined for students.

Heterogeneous grouping is desired in individualised programmes of reading instruction. Regardless of achievement and interest levels, each student can select sequential those library books which meet personal needs, interests, and abilities.

**Language Experience Methods**

Language experience approaches in teaching reading emphasise content to be read which comes from the personal experiences of involved students. Too frequently, students read content from textbooks which does not relate to their personal lives. Thus, to initiate and develop a language experience reading curriculum, learners need to have rich personal experiences. These experiences may include the use of excursions on the school grounds and into the larger community, films, filmstrips, slides, illustrations, transparencies and the overhead, and games/simulations.

Pertaining to the language experience method in teaching reading, Bush and Huebner wrote:

In the initial stages when children dictate their own stories, the teacher as recorder points out letters that stand for sounds, good words the children have used to express their ideas, and sentence structure. He or she helps the child note similarities in beginning and ending of some words and helps the children build a basic stock of sight vocabulary useful in their reading and writing.

Meaningful experiences with clay, paint, and other materials provide opportunities for further self-expression. As children spontaneously talk about their activities, they are encouraged to write their own stories. They write again in content areas as they record information on topics of interest, contributing to class newspapers or class books. The teacher encourages self-expression and helps children as they ask for spelling, punctuation marks, and other aids to writing. Reading practice is obtained as children read their own writing, each other's, and, finally, the adult writing in published material.

Language experience approaches do not emphasise:

1. The use of textbooks and workbooks in teaching Teading;
2. Utilisation of behaviourally stated ends in teaching and learning;
3. A formal, teacher determined reading curriculum;
4. Homogeneous grouping procedures in reading;
5. Commercially prepared materials in teaching reading.

## Interage Grouping

Interage grouping advocates believe that learners of several age levels should be taught as a group in reading. This harmonises more with life in society in which individuals of several age levels interact with each other. Educators emphasising interage grouping state that a single age level of learners in a classroom does not, by any means, guarantee homogeneity in the classroom. A cross age group may be more homogeneous in reading ability as compared to a set of students basically having the same/similar chronological age. Thus, students in grades four, five, and six may be regrouped so that the highest achievers in reading are in one classroom, the next best achievers in the second classroom, the third best achievers in the third room, and so on. The chances are that in any one classroom, there will be students from grades, four, five, and six.

Interage grouping does not stress:

1. Learners of a single chronological age being taught together continuously;
2. separating the school environment from society in terms of age levels;
3. heterogeneous grouping in the reading curriculum;
4. learners meeting grade level standards, based on the individual grade level they are in presently;
5. the self contained classroom, in which a given set of students is being taught continuously in all curriculum areas.

## Heterogeneous Grouping in Reading

Numerous educators recommend heterogeneous grouping of students in the classroom. Mixed achievement and capacity levels of learners are then inherent in a given set of learners. The gifted and slower learners may be taught in separate groups in a homogeneous setting. Many reading specialists believe that within a heterogeneous group, the teacher can provide for increased uniformity in achievement within a set of students by grouping learners homogeneously. Thus, three reading groups may be an end result within a room—the fast, the average, and the slower readers.

Pertaining to heterogeneous grouping, Shepherd and Regan wrote:

Heterogeneous instructional groups or classes are formed whenever no single factor governs the assignment of pupils to groups and classes. Heterogeneous classes are viewed as containing the same ranges of instructional and individual differences as the total group at that position on the vertical sequence.

## Advantages Claimed for Heterogeneous Grouping

1. The interaction of the various ability levels contributes to all aspects of development and achievement;
2. Heterogeneous groups are more analogous to the relationships in life;
3. The instructional models and participation alternatives available to pupils and teachers are more numerous;
4. Some research studies generally favour social, affective, and maturational advantages for children in heterogeneous groups.

## Limitations Claimed for Heterogeneous Grouping

1. The research evidence concerning achievement generally suggest that there are no differences between the two grouping plans.
2. The wider range of variations in achievement needs and capacities make it difficult for the teacher to provide for the individualisation of instruction.
3. The pupils who learn more slowly are less likely to have opportunities for academic leadership and success because of the presence of brighter pupils.

### Heterogeneous Grouping does not Emphasise

1. Grouping top achievers in reading in one classroom, the next best achievers in a second room, followed by succeeding levels of slower achievers in other rooms.
2. Tracking learners within a classroom in terms of ability levels. Each student, however, must be guided to achieve optimally in reading.
3. A certain ability level of students learning from each other only, in a classroom. Rather, students of mixed achievement levels are to learn from each other.

### Programmed Reading Instruction

Each student achieves on an individual basis when utilising programmed materials. In using programmed textbooks, the programmer selects objectives for students to attain. Thus, the programmer chooses sequential learnings for learners. A small amount of content is presented to the involved student when reading from a programmed text. Next the learner answers a completion item covering the subject matter read. Generally, the response is written by the student in a separate answer book. Next, the learner uncovers the correct answer to the completion item as provided by the programmer. If the student responded correctly, reinforcement in learning should be in evidence and the learner is ready for the next sequential programmed item. No grouping of students is necessary. Each achieves at his own unique optimal rate. Should the involved student have responded incorrectly, he/she sees the correct answer as provided by the programmer and is still ready for the next sequential linear item in reading. The same/similar procedure in learning is used again and again—read, respond, and the check by the involved learner.

Pertaining to programmed instruction, Skinner wrote:

An important contribution has been the so-called "programming" of knowledge and skills—the construction of carefully arranged sequences of contingencies leading to the terminal performances which are the object of education. The teacher begins with whatever behaviour the student brings to the instructional situation; by selective reinforcement, he changes that behaviour so that a given terminal performance is more and more closely approximated. Even with lower organisms, quite complex behaviours can be "shaped" in this way with surprising speed; the human organism is presumably far more sensitive. So important is the principle of programming that it is often regarded as the main contribution of the teaching-machine movement, but the experimental analysis of behaviour has much more to contribute to a technology of education.

Computer Assisted Instruction (CAI) works in a similar manner as is true of using programmed textbooks. At a computer terminal center, the student, working on an individual basis, types in his/her name on the keyboard. The appropriate lesson number also needs to be typed in. The first item for the student to read appears on the monitor or screen. A small amount of subject matter appears on the screen. This is followed by a question to answer or a completion item to complete. The involved student types in the intended correct response. If the learner responded correctly, he/she is rewarded with the statement "that's good" appearing on the screen. The student is then ready for the next sequential linear item. If an incorrect response was given by the student, the words "try again" may appear on the screen. If a correct response to the same item is then given by the student, he/she progresses to the next sequential item. If incorrect, the learner now sees the correct response on the screen and is also ready for the next sequential task. Continually, the learner reads, responds, and checks using CAI in ordered, sequential steps of learning, Wohlwill wrote:

It is interesting to note the fascination which subject matter characterised by a high degree of internal structure, such as mathematics, logic, and the physical sciences, have exerted on those active in the field of programming. These are, of course, precisely the subjects which lend themselves most readily to the construction of programmes consisting of a national sequence of small steps. Once this ladder has been built for the learner, it is assumed that he will inexorably move upward by dint of successive reinforcements. Thus, the need for any further attention to the learning process involved in the mastery of the material by the student is apparently obviated.

It may be noted in passing that this approach implicitly takes for granted the intervention of certain verbal and mediational processes in the learner, whose role in the learning process is hardly recognised, let alone understood. One may well ask by what magic the logical or semantic relations between successive items in a sequence built by the programmer are in fact responded to by the learner. That he may do so (provided he has reached the appropriate level of verbal and intellectual development, and the programmer has done his work skillfully and diligently enough) is an undeniable empirical fact, but until some attempt is made to investigate just what the learner does in proceeding along such a sequence, this will remain a purely pragmatic enterprise, built essentially on guesswork.

## In Closing

There are numerous means of grouping students for reading instruction. Each plan needs to be studied thoroughly in terms of strengths and weaknesses. Ultimately, a method or combination of methods need selecting to guide each student to achieve as well as possible in reading.

## REFERENCES

1. Bush, Clifford L. and Margaret Huebner. *Strategies for Reading in the Elementary School*. Second Edition. New York: Macmillan Publishing Company, 1979.
2. Dufay, Frank R. *Ungrading the Elementary School*. West Nyack, New York: Parker Publishing Company, 1966.
3. Ediger, Marlow. *Relevancy in Elementary Curriculum*. Kirksville Missouri: Simpson Publishing Company, 1975.
4. Shepherd, Gene D. and William B. Ragan. *Modern Elementary Curriculum*. Sixth Edition. New York, Rinehart and Winston, 1982.
5. Skinner, B.F. "Reflections on a Decade of Teaching Machines", *Teachers College Record*, November, 1963.

6. Veatch, Jeanette. *Individualising your Reading Programme*. New York: G.P. Putnam's Sons, 1959.

7. Wohlwill, Joachim. "The Teaching Machine: Psychology's New Hobbyhorse," *Teacher's College Record*, November, 1962.

# Classical Poetry in the School Setting

Too frequently, modern poetry only, is studied by pupils in school. There, no doubt, should be a balance between classical and modern poetry. There are a plethora of reasons for studying classical poetry. This is poetry which has stood the test of time, over the years. The exact time interval cannot be pinpointed, but the chances are these poets are no longer living. The writings, not deemed to have merit will, in most situations, have faded from importance. This is not to say that some of these may not be resurrected again. But, classical writings do remain in saliency as the years go by.

It is important to notice which authors and their respective poems survive. Students need to learn about the style of writing of classical poets. The subject matter or content in the classical poems needs to be discussed. Students need to learn about the style and ideas written about. Times change and yet there is a richness about classical poetry which has survived in importance.

We did notice that few of my undergraduate and graduate students could recite or remember few titles of poems, let alone recite their contents. One of our colleagues, older than us, lamented that university students were unable to recite classical poems. He was able to recite, enthusiastically, many poems by memory and had a book of classical poetry on his desk top for rather frequent reference. We do feel that classical poetry is refreshing and relaxing to read and study on my own. When attending the public schools, the classics were strongly emphasised in literature classes. Rarely were modern writings stressed. As a freshman in college, modern literature only was studied in class. I barely remember any of the contents in the writings. We do recall that the contents, in general, dealt largely with what veterans of World War II experienced while in military service and what their goals were after being discharged. Somehow, the subject matter in these writings did not impress me. This might well be a personal matter, but there are those seemingly who do prefer literature which has proven its worth in time and space.

## Classical Writings for Teachers

Henry Van Dyke (1852-1933), an American clergyman, educator, novelist, essayist, statesman, and poet, wrote the following in poetic form:

And what is teaching? Ah! There you have the worst paid and the best rewarded of all vocations. Dare not enter it unless you love it. For the vast majority of men for whom it has no promise for wealth or fame but they to whom it is dear for its own sake are among the nobility of mankind. I sing the praise of the unknown teacher, king of himself and leader of mankind! (See Ratna Papa, 1997).

Dr. Herman Harrell Horne (1874-1946) was an educational philosopher at New York University. He was a prolific writer of journal articles and education textbooks on idealism as a philosophy of education. The following writing of Dr. Horne follows the Sermon on the Mount (Matthew 5-7) pattern:

*Blessed are you teachers:* For you have found your work.

*Blessed are you teachers:* For you are freed from the temptation to put your trust in money.

*Blessed are you teachers:* For yours is the kingdom of children.

*Blessed are you teachers:* For your associates are among the world's best.

*Blessed are you teachers:* For your work is constantly realising your selfhood.

*Blessed are you teachers:* For you may 'allure to brighter worlds' of truth and live and learn the way.

*Blessed are you teachers:* For you have kinship with the great sharing of souls of all mankind.

*Blessed are you teachers:* For you have an Elder Brother who is the Great Teacher, even of the whole world (See Wahlquist, 1942).

Ralph Waldo Emerson (1803-1882), wrote many well known books and essays during his life time. His writings, in many cases, tended to emphasise encouraging others in their daily pursuits. Emerson experienced many tragedies in life including the death of his father at age eight, a younger brother was mentally retarded, another was mentally ill and died in 1834, while a third brother died of tuberculosis in 1836. Emerson's first wife died in 1831. And yet, one of his greatest writings dealt in self reliance:

Trust thyself; every heart vibrates to that iron string. Accept the place the divine providence has found for you, the society of your contemporaries, the connection of events. Great men have always done so, and confided themselves childlike to the genius of their age, betraying their perception that the almighty trustworthy was seated at their heart, working though their hands, predominating in all their being. And we are now men, and must accept the highest mind the same transcendent destiny, and not minors or invalids in a protected corner, not cowards fleeing before a revolution but guides, redeemers, and beneficiaries, obeying the Almighty effort and advancing on Chaos and the Dark... Whoever would be a man must be a nonconformist. He who would gather immortal psalm must not be hindered by the name of goodness. Nothing is at last sacred but the integrity of your own mind (Whicher, Editor, 1957).*

Each of the above writings are essays and written in poetic form. Henry Van Dyke expresses truths pertaining to teaching with its low pay and yet it being of immense worth. Individuals should not enter teaching unless it is truly valued. Van Dyke does indeed extol the virtues of teaching as leaders in society.

Herman Harrell Horne specifies why teaching is important and uses verse to express his ideas. His writing is based upon a classical selection—The Sermon on the Mount. He, too, stressed that teachers did not enter the profession for the purpose of becoming wealthy, but there are a plethora of other values such as working with children, with other professionals, and being of great value to society.

Ralph Waldo Emerson believed strongly in the capacity of human beings to do what is good. He was very optimistic in life, even though his life had been filled with extreme difficulties. Emerson emphasised that people trust themselves. He is very poetic in describing the lot of human beings in life's situations. Lean upon thyself was a key admonition that Emerson gave to others.

*Frequently at educational meetings and conventions, a speaker will draw upon lines of verse which has inspirational value for classroom teachers. Henry Van Dyke, Herman Harrell Horne, and Ralph Waldo Emerson, among others, have much to contribute, as classical writers, for teachers presently. These three writers emphasised the importance of teachers and the influence each teacher has upon others. Teachers truly must be a dedicated set of professionals who value working with young people and who must value what they do for its very own sake.

* Note Emerson uses masculine terms in some of his writings, but these can be noted and substitutions made with nouns/pronouns which refer to both genders.

## Classical Poetry in the Curriculum

The classical poems included the Vision of Sir Launfal by James Russell Lowell (1819-1891). The plot of the poem relates directly to the times of King Arthur's reign when the search for the Holy Grail was emphasised. He begins the poem with the following:

And what is so rare as the days in June,
Then, if ever come perfect days

Then heaven tries earth if it be in tune and over it softly her warm ear lies.

Here, Lowell makes a creative comparison, using the smile "as" between the month of June and its perfection. In poetic language, he describes the month of June in the novel use of language with heaven trying earth to see if it is in tune with excellence. Scientific content is not inherent in the writing. Poetry, however, can relate to science in the writer describing early summer, a season of the year.

Morality is mentioned in the *Vision of Sir Launfal* with the following:

Who gives himself with Alms feeds three—
Himself, his hungering neighbour, and me.

With good citizenship being a major objective for students to achieve, giving of one's time, talents, and money to needy people may well be a highly virtuous thing to do, not only during holiday seasons, but throughout the year. The writer of this poem uses rhyme to indicate the goodness of giving, *three* and *me*.

Philosophy, one of the social sciences, may be stressed developmentally for student understanding with the following creative lines from the same poem:

Joy comes, grief goes
We know not how.

The above phenomenon is interesting to speculate on. Sometimes, it appears as if one works for joy to come and grief to go. But at the same time, the plans may well go awry. At other times, it appears to be predetermined for some individuals to experience much of the positive in life. Selected individuals in society experience more of the good things than do others. Thus, in suburbia, it appears that things go very well for most. Or might it just appear that way in many cases? James Russell Lowell wrote:

Now the heart is so full that a drop over fills it.
We are happy because God wills it.

These two lines of verse indicate that a supernatural force is the cause of happiness, not the effort of the person, nor are chance factors involved. Rhyme is used to show the cause, including the words *fills* and *wills*. All poetry is to be enjoyed and read silently as well as aloud. Students should be encouraged to list their favourite vocabulary found in poems as well as record metaphors and similes noticed. Journaling is a good way for students to do these writings as well as develop a list of favourite poems. We noticed when supervising university student teachers in the public schools that pupils developed their own booklet of favourite poems. This included classical as well as modern poetry. When emphasis is placed upon studying and writing poems. We felt these students were highly interested in poems and their respective authors. In these public school classrooms, there were student poetry writings on the classroom bulletin board, posted in hallways outside the classroom door, the teacher had an anthology of poems on his/her classroom desk, and a bound copy of poetry written by pupils for all to read in the classroom library. In one classroom, each pupil kept a folder of poems written to be bound at the end of a semester. The cover of each had a title and the pupil's name as author.

Oliver Wendell Holmes (1809-1894) wrote a well known poem in 1830 entitled "Old Ironsides." Old Ironsides, actually named "The Constitution," was written in response to its proposed being dismantled. This ship was deemed outdated and not fit for service. Holmes felt strongly about preserving the Constitution, and it still exists today when it was towed to Boston Harbor in 1997 for its permanent home. The first stanza of "Old Ironsides" reveals the strong feelings and emotions Oliver Wendell Holmes had toward the dismantling of the ship.

Ay, Tear her tattered ensign down!
Long has it waved on high,
and many an eye has danced to see
That Banner in the key.
Beneath it rung the battle shout
and burst the cannon's roar.
The meteor of the ocean air
Shall sweep the clouds nor more...

It is always important for students to learn background information of the poem as well as about the author's life and times. These experiences can be highly interesting to students and assist them to attach meaning to the poem. Old Ironsides should be read aloud with voice intonation and inflection, as well as with prosody. Oliver Wendell Holmes had strong feelings in that Old Ironsides should be preserved. Students need to notice the creative use of language and indicate which words/ phrases capture their attention. Rhyme should be noticed, realising that not all poems contain rhyming words.

There are a plethora of poems which may be directly related to historical units of study and Old Ironsides comes in that category.

Henry Wadsworth Longfellow (1807-1882) is known for many written poems which have survived in time and space. He is revered for writing The Children's Hour, The Courtship of Miles Standish, Song of Hiawatha, and Paul Revere's ride, among many others. Longfellow reveals his love for children with his poem, "The Children's Hour." Children love to listen to this writing when it is read aloud with appropriate stress, pitch, an juncture:

Between the dark and the daylight,
When the night is beginning to lower,
Comes a pause in the day's occupations,
That is known as the Children's Hour.

I hear in the chamber above me
The patter of little feet,
The sound of a door that is opened,
And voices soft and sweet.
From my study in the lamplight,
Descending the broad hall stair,
Grave Alice and laughing Allegra,
and Edith with Golden Hair...

Longfellow was able to take an every day occurrence and develop it into a beautiful poem. He describes in detail with beautiful words in poetic manner how children are attracted to him and he to children. Longfellow is the only American to be entombed in Westminster Abbey in London, England.

### In Closing

Classical writing have a beauty in language of their very own. They have stood evaluations of their goodness as the years have come and gone. Students do like good teaching and they do love enduring writings known as the classics! The classical poems in this manuscript are only a beginning in having pupils study the works of those poets, men and women, whose works are enduring.

## REFERENCES

Ediger, Marlow (1998), *Reading and the Language Arts*. Kirksville, Missouri: Simpson Publishing Company.

Papa, C. Ratna (1997), *The Personal Satisfaction and Professional Satisfaction of Women Teachers*, Tirupati 517 502, A.P., India: University of Baroda, 22.

Wahlquist, John T. (1942), *The Philosophy of American Education*, New York: Ronald Press Company: 386.

Whicher, Stephen E. (Editor, 1957), Selections from Ralph Waldo Emerson. Boston: Houghton, Mifflin Company, 148-149.

# Special Education Students and Mandated Objectives

There certainly is a major problem in having special students meet state mandated objectives. Special education students here will refer to the handicapped, English Language Learners (ELL), English as a Second Language (ESL), and students from minority groups. These students are to meet state mandated objectives as are the regular students in the classroom. Special education students have not had the opportunities that other learners have experienced. And yet, they are to achieve as well as others. When viewing state mandated test results, the special education students are viewed in separate categories to notice if they, too, are meeting mandated standards.

**Should they be Assessed in the Same Manner?**

Special education students have lacked opportunities which other learners have had, such as in the following ways:

1. Handicapped students include the visually and hearing impaired as well as the mentally retarded;
2. ELL students who are learning the English language presently but are being tested in the English language;
3. ESL students who speak another language much more fluently as compared to English;
4. Minority students due to experiencing poverty have not had the chances to achieve due to limited financial resources.

It hardly seems fair to assess special education students with the same standards as those who are more favoured with having grown up speaking the English language as well as having more beneficial ability and economic resources. But, they do need to be assessed in some manner to determine educational achievement. The best objectives, learning opportunities to achieve the objectives, and assessment procedures need to be available to special education students.

The playing field is not level, by any means, when testing normal students with those in special education categories. Special education students may be helped with high quality developmentally appropriate learning opportunities whereby concrete, semiconcrete, and abstract learnings are provided on their present level of achievement. Sequentially, students need to achieve as optimally as possible Assessment procedures include not only state mandated testing but also teacher developed informal evaluations. State mandated testing is terminal whereas teacher developed tests are formative assisting students along the way to do better on state mandated tests.

## Absolute Versus Value Added Assessments

Special education students have been required to achieve absolute standards. The state mandated tests, being terminal, are used to ascertain if students should be promoted in grades three through eight and grade ten. With summative evaluation, a student either does or does not pass the mandated test. There are no exceptions made. All students in a grade take the same test and are provided with the same directions for test taking. No allowances are made for special education students in test taking. When giving a teacher written test, allowances may be made in terms of time limits, pronouncing unknown words, and even ways of responding to a test item. When responding to a teacher written test item, the test taker would not need to fill in a bubble, punch a computerised card, or take the test online. With teacher written tests, the student may draw a picture, a diagram, or make a chart to indicate what has been learned. What does a test measure if:

1. a student cannot read in the English language?
2. a student lacks needed abilities in reading?
3. a student has not had opportunities to learn which suburban learners have had?

In measuring adequate yearly progress (ayp), those schools having the most ELL, ESL, minorities, and handicapped students will do worse than schools from very favourably home and school environments. Also, those schools having fewer than thirty students in any one category, will not be considered when determining the ayp.

Having all special education students achieve value added standards would make more sense. With value added, each special education student is measured against his/her previous test performance, not against absolute standards. Measuring a student's progress from previous to present times would indicate the amount of achievement made, be it individually to be promoted from one grade level to the next or to be incorporated into the ayp. For any one student, what has been achieved from one measurement to the next is what is salient. Absolute standards may be too busy for some and too difficult for others. Value added standards then measure:

1. to notice achievement of a student as a result of instruction;
2. to notice the amount of student achievement in yearly testing;
3. to notice how value added instruction affects ayp;
4. to better diagnose and remedy individual student progress as a result of value added testing;
5. to notice how valued added testing compares with absolute standards of measurement.

Value added testing makes comparison of the individuals present achievement as compared to an earlier measure. Absolute standards make comparisons among individuals as to how well each is doing. Absolute standards makes comparisons of how well a student is achieving the predetermined state mandated objectives, as revealed through testing. Absolute standards in determining ayp compares this year's students with those of last year. Cohort groups are then used in making these comparisons since last year's and this year's comparison groups are not the same students.

## Additional Accepted Approaches in Assessments

No school or school system should conceive of state mandated testing as being the only way of assessment. Teachers may also write tests which are valid and reliable. When using face validity, the teacher may write a test item which relates directly to what just has been taught. By doing this, the teacher does not forget what has been taught when writing a test items. Notes may be made or a check placed on the lesson plan on what has been taught. After school or during break time, the teacher may write the test item and also preserve test security. If test items are written very clearly by following recommendations of measurement specialist, reliability might well be more in evidence than would otherwise be the case. The teacher cannot give the same test to the same students to ascertain test/retest reliability, but he/she may use split half reliability. Split half reliability requires giving the test once only. Then split half reliability may then be determined.

Too frequently, only multiple choice test items are used on state mandated tests. With teacher written test, there is a better chance of using essay tests measuring higher levels of cognition. Essay tests, will written and edited, might well measure skills in problem solving, as well as critical and creative thinking. To assess essay test results more objectively, the teacher may develop and use a rubric. The rubric pinpoints what the teacher is looking for in essay test results. Thus, it objectifies what is being evaluated. All tests have elements of subjectivity involved. State mandated tests then have standard errors of measurement which indicate margin of error. It indicates the range within which any student score may fall. A student, for example, received a score of sixty on a test. The standard error of measurement, statistically arrived at, may reveal three score points. The student's true score may then be in the range of

60 + 3 and 60 – 3. Errors in test construction make for a statistically computed standard error of measurement.

State mandated testing involves summative evaluation. The test score for the student represents the end of the instructional year. Teacher written tests generally emphasise formative evaluation, unless it is given at the end of an instructional sequence or unit of study. With formative evaluation, the teacher receives feedback from the student as to what has/has not been learned. What has not been learned provides information to the teacher as to what still needs to be taught and retaught. In addition to essay tests and multiple choice test items, the teacher needs to use observation of daily student performance. Here, the teacher notices problems which students have in learning and achievement. Diagnosis and remediation might then be in the offing.

## Recommendations on State Mandated Testing

There are a plethora of recommendations which might be made in improving evaluation of student progress. First, there needs to be accommodations for special education students. These accommodations may pertain to the difficulty of the test, the length of the test, and assistance given during test taking. Second, additional procedures of assessment need to be in the offing other than a single test score to determine promotion from one grade level to the next and for receiving a high school diploma. Portfolios, projects completed, and teacher recommendations should also be a part of the assessment procedures. Third, high validity and reliability for state written tests need to be in the offing, otherwise the test may have little value in ascertaining learner achievement. Thus through pilot testing is recommendable, resulting in the kinks being taken out of the test. Fourth, accuracy in computer scoring needs to be assessed so that student irregularities of results do not occur. There have been too many nightmares about computer scoring errors. Fifth, the length of a state mandated test needs to be such as to avoid student fatigue in test taking. Sixth, state mandated tests need to be diagnostic in nature so that teachers may receive feedback on how to assist students in learning.

Sixth, students should receive necessary, accommodations which harmonise with disabilities involved. Seventh, directions given for test taking should be very clear. Vague directions for test taking do not help in ascertaining how much students have learned. Eight, experimentation should be done to find multiple ways for students to respond to test items. Multiple intelligences theory indicates that each student has a preference in indicating what has been learned. Not all responses should involve filling in a bubble to show what has been learned. Art work, making a diagram, or pointing to an answer should also be an alternative. Ninth, styles of learning might well provide additional information to determine under which conditions students learn best. There are students who work best individually whereas others prefer cooperative endeavours. Selected evaluations may include student preference in learning be it intrapersonal versus interpersonal. Tenth, state mandated, as well as other forms of evaluation, should include items and observations including the following:

(a) caring for others;

(b) working harmoniously with others;

(c) thinking critically and creatively;

(d) solving identified problems;

(e) assisting peers when needed;

(f) modelling good study habits;

(g) persevering through difficulties;

(h) cultivating good listening habits;

(i) speaking clearly so all can hear;

(j) doing neat school work and stressing neatness in all significant endeavours;

(k) being able to do school work well which is developmentally appropriate.

## Conclusion

Special education students need a developmentally suited curriculum whereby sequential progress might will be in

**evidence. Suitable objectives, learning activities which make for success in learning, and assessment procedures which are valid and reliable making for a successful special education curriculum.**

## REFERENCES


Astin, P. and C. Buxton (2000), "Science as Inquiry", *Boblinks*, 10 (2), 10-15.

Blough, Glenn O., and Julius Schwartz (1984), *Elementary School Science and How to Teach It*. New York: CBS College Publishing.

Condrey, Jean Friend (1996), "Focus on Science Concepts", *The Science Teacher*, 63 (4).

Dewey, John (1916), *Democracy and Education*. New York: The Macmillan Company.

Ediger, Marlow (1999). *Teaching Science in the Elementary School*. Kirksville, Missouri: Simpson Publishing Company, Chapter Seven.

—— (1995), "Designing Science Units of Study," *School Science*, 33 (1), 14-15.

Melber, Leah M. (2003), *"True Tales of Science,"* Science and Children 41 (2), 24-32.

National Research Council (1996), *National Science Education Standards*, Washington, DC: National Academy Press.

Ward, Kathleen, et. al. (1996), "Constructing Scientific Knowledge," *The Science Teacher*, 63 (9).

Wolf, Kenneth (1996), "Developing an Effective Teaching Portfolio", *Educational Leadership*, 53; 34.

# Additional Reading

Bhaskara Rao, Digumarti (1994). *Scientific Aptitude*. New Delhi: Ashish Publishing House. ISBN 81-7024-658-X.

Bhaskara Rao, Digumarti (1995). *Animal Kingdom*. New Delhi: Discovery Publishing House. ISBN 81-7141-274-2.

Bhaskara Rao, Digumarti (1995). *Batracology*. New Delhi: Discovery Publishing House. ISBN 81-7141-279-3.

Bhaskara Rao, Digumarti (1997). *Scientific Attitude*. New Delhi: Discovery Publishing House. ISBN 81-7141-381-1.

Bhaskara Rao, Digumarti (1996). *Scientific Attitude vis-à-vis Scientific Aptitude*. New Delhi: Discovery Publishing House. ISBN 81-7141-308-0.

Bhaskara Rao, Digumarti (2004). *Scientific Attitude, Scientific Aptitude and Achievement*. New Delhi: Discovery Publishing House. ISBN 81-7141-781-7.

Bhaskara Rao, Digumarti (2004). *Educational Administration*. New Delhi: Discovery Publishing House. ISBN 81-7141-842-2.

Bhaskara Rao, Digumarti, editor (1996). *Encyclopaedia of Education For All*, 5 volumes. New Delhi: APH Publishing Corporation. ISBN 81-7024-759-4 (set).

Vol. I *Education For All: The World Conference*. ISBN 81-7024-760-8.

Vol. II *Education For All: The EPA-9 Summit*. ISBN 81-7024-761-6.

Vol. III *Education For All: Quality Education For All.* ISBN 81-7024-762-6.

Vol. IV *Education For All: Planning and Monitoring.* ISBN 81-7024-763-4.

Vol. V *Education For All: The Indian Scenario.* ISBN 81-7024-764-0.

Bhaskara Rao, Digumarti, editor (1996). *Global Perceptions on Peace Education*, 3 volumes. New Delhi: Discovery Publishing House. ISBN 81-7141-319-6.

Bhaskara Rao, Digumarti, editor (1996). *National Policy on Education*, 2 volumes. New Delhi: Anmol Publications Pvt. Ltd. ISBN 81-7488-323-1.

Bhaskara Rao, Digumarti, editor (1997). *Care the Child*, 2 volumes. New Delhi: Discovery Publishing House. ISBN 81-7141-394-3.

Bhaskara Rao, Digumarti, editor (1997). *Education for the 21st Century*. New Delhi: Discovery Publishing House. ISBN 81-7141-389-7.

Bhaskara Rao, Digumarti, editor (1997). *Reflections on Scientific Attitude*. New Delhi: Discovery Publishing House. ISBN 81-7141-319-6.

Bhaskara Rao, Digumarti, editor (1997). *Success Story of a Primary Education Project*. New Delhi: APH Publishing Corporation. ISBN 81-7024-850-7.

Bhaskara Rao, Digumarti, editor (1997). *World Food Summit.* New Delhi: Discovery Publishing House. ISBN 81-7141-386-2.

Bhaskara Rao, Digumarti, editor (1998). *Adolescence Education.* New Delhi: Discovery Publishing House. ISBN 81-7141-432-X.

Bhaskara Rao, Digumarti, editor (1998). *Community and School Nutrition Education*. New Delhi: Discovery Publishing House. ISBN 81-7141-435-4.

Bhaskara Rao, Digumarti, editor (1998). *District Primary Education Programme*. New Delhi: Discovery Publishing House. ISBN 81-7141-396-X.

Bhaskara Rao, Digumarti, editor (1998). *Earth Summit*, 2 volumes. New Delhi: Discovery Publishing House. ISBN 81-7141-435-4.

Bhaskara Rao, Digumarti, editor (1998). *National Policy on Education: Towards an Enlightened and Humane Society*. New Delhi: Discovery Publishing House. ISBN 81-7141-426-5.

Bhaskara Rao, Digumarti, editor (1998). *Reforming School Education*. New Delhi: Discovery Publishing House. ISBN 81-7141-403-6.

Bhaskara Rao, Digumarti, editor (1998). *Teacher Education in India*. New Delhi: Discovery Publishing House. ISBN 81-7141-406-0.

Bhaskara Rao, Digumarti, editor (1998). *World Summit for Social Development*. New Delhi: Discovery Publishing House. ISBN 81-7141-420-6.

Bhaskara Rao, Digumarti, editor (2000). *Education For All: Achieving the Goal*, 3 volumes. New Delhi: APH Publishing Corporation. ISBN 81-7648-152-1 (set).

Vol. I *The Global Consensus*. ISBN 81-7648-155-6.

Vol. II *Mid-Decade Review Reports of Regional Seminars*. ISBN 81-7648-154-8.

Vol. III *Issues and Trends*. ISBN 81-7648-155-6.

Bhaskara Rao, Digumarti, editor (1999). *International Encyclopaedia of AIDS*, 11 volumes. New Delhi: Discovery Publishing House. ISBN 81-7141-522-6 (set).

Vol. 1 *Introduction to HIV/AIDS*. ISBN 81-7141-523-7.

Vol. 2 *HIV/AIDS-Issues and Challenges*, 2 parts. ISBN 81-7141-524-5.

Vol. 3 *HIV/AIDS-Socio Economic Realities*. ISBN 81-7141-524-3.

Vol. 4 *HIV/AIDS-Law Ethics and Human Rights*, 2 parts. ISBN 81-7141-526-1.

Vol. 5 *AIDS and NGOs*. ISBN 81-7141-527-X.

Vol. 6 *AIDS and Home Care*. ISBN 81-7141-528-8.

Vol. 7 *STD Case Management*. ISBN 81-7141-529-6.

Vol. 8 *HIV/AIDS Prevention and Care-Teaching Modules for Nurses and Midwives*. ISBN 81-7141-530-X.

Vol. 9 *HIV Prevention Education for Educational Institutions*. ISBN 81-7141-531-8.

Vol.10 *Instructional Modules for AIDS Education*. ISBN 81-7141-532-6.

Vol.11 *School Health Education to Prevent AIDS and STD-A Package for Curriculum Planners*. ISBN 81-7141-533-4.

Bhaskara Rao, Digumarti, editor (2000). *International Encyclopaedia of Science and Technology Education*, 11 volumes. New Delhi: Discovery Publishing House. ISBN 81-7141-548-2 (set).

Vol. 1 *Science and Technology Education*. ISBN 81-7141-568-7.

Vol. 2 *Science Education in Developing Countries*. ISBN 81-7141-569-9.

Vol. 3 *Organizational Structure of Science*. ISBN 81-7141-570-9.

Vol. 4 *Science Education in Asia and the Pacific*. ISBN 81-7141-571-7

Vol. 5 *Science and Technology Education For All*. ISBN 81-7141-572-5.

Vol. 6 *Values, Ethics, Talent and Girls in Science and Technology Education*. ISBN 81-7141-573-3.

Vol. 7 *Popularization of Science and Technology Education*. ISBN 81-7141-574-1.

Vol. 8 *Science, Power and Society*. ISBN 81-7141-575-X.

Vol. 9 *Information Technology*. ISBN 81-7141-576-8.

Vol. 10 *Teacher Training in Science and Technology Education*. ISBN 81-7142-577-6.

Vol. 11 *Teacher Training in Science and Technology: A Curriculum Framework*. ISBN 81-7141-578-4.

Bhaskara Rao, Digumarti, editor (2001). *Distance Education in Different Countries*. New Delhi: APH Publishing Corporation. ISBN 81-7648-229-3.

Bhaskara Rao, Digumarti, editor (2001). *Decentralised Management of Education: Management of Education in Panchayati Raj and Municipal Bodies*. New Delhi: Discovery Publishing House. ISBN 81-7141-617-9.

Bhaskara Rao, Digumarti, editor (2001). *Electrochemistry for Environmental Protection*. New Delhi: Discovery Publishing House. ISBN 81-7141-619-5.

Bhaskara Rao, Digumarti, editor (2001). *Global Educational Studies*. New Delhi: Discovery Publishing House. ISBN 81-7141-616-0.

Bhaskara Rao, Digumarti, editor (2001). *Global Synthesis of Educational Assessment*. New Delhi: Discovery Publishing House. ISBN 81-7141-613-6.

Bhaskara Rao, Digumarti, editor (2000). *International Encyclopaedia of Human Rights*, 7 volumes in 13 parts. New Delhi: Discovery Publishing House. ISBN 81-7141-567-9 (set).

Vol. 1 *International Instruments of Human Rights*, 2 parts. ISBN 81-7141-569-4.

Vol. 2 *Regional Instruments of Human Rights*. ISBN 81-7141-604-7.

Vol. 3 *Human Rights and the United Nations*, 2 parts. ISBN 81-7141-605-5.

Vol. 4 *Fact Files of Human Rights*, 3 parts. ISBN 81-7141-606-3.

Vol. 5 *Study Stories of Human Rights*, 3 parts. ISBN 81-7141-607-3.

Vol. 6 *International Meetings on Human Rights*, 2 parts. ISBN 81-714-608-X.

Vol. 7 *Professional Training in Human Rights*. ISBN 81-7141-609-8.

Bhaskara Rao, Digumarti, editor (2001). *Jomtein Decade of Education*. New Delhi: Discovery Publishing House. ISBN 81-7141-618-7.

Bhaskara Rao, Digumarti, editor (2001). *Nuclear Materials: Issues and Concerns*, 2 volumes. New Delhi: Discovery Publishing House. ISBN 81-7141-611-X.

Bhaskara Rao, Digumarti, editor (2001). *World Conference on Education for All*. New Delhi: APH Publishing Corporation. ISBN 81-7141-274-9.

Bhaskara Rao, Digumarti, editor (2001). *World Conference on Higher Education*. New Delhi: Discovery Publishing House. ISBN 81-7141-610-1.

Bhaskara Rao, Digumarti, editor (2001). *World Conference on Science*. New Delhi: Discovery Publishing House. ISBN 81-7141-612-8.

Bhaskara Rao, Digumarti, editor (2003). *Inspiring Experiences in Teacher Education*. New Delhi: Discovery Publishing House. ISBN 81-7141-656-X.

Bhaskara Rao, Digumarti, editor (2003). *International Studies in Education*, 3 volumes. New Delhi: Discovery Publishing House. ISBN 81-7141-647-0.

Bhaskara Rao, Digumarti, editor (2003). *Military Conversion: Impact on Science and Technology*. New Delhi: Discovery Publishing House. ISBN 81-7141-578-4.

Bhaskara Rao, Digumarti, editor (2003). *United Nations Millennium Summit*. New Delhi: Discovery Publishing House. ISBN 81-7141-632-2.

Bhaskara Rao, Digumarti, editor (2003). *World Assembly on Aging. New Delhi*: Discovery Publishing House. ISBN 81-7141-637-3.

Bhaskara Rao, Digumarti, editor (2003). *World Conference on Human Rights*. New Delhi: Discovery Publishing House. ISBN 81-7141-661-6.

Bhaskara Rao, Digumarti, editor (2003). *World Education Forum*. New Delhi: Discovery Publishing House. ISBN 81-7141-639-X.

Bhaskara Rao, Digumarti, editor (2003). *Education, Employment and Human Resource Development*. New Delhi: Discovery Publishing House. ISBN 81-7141-681-0.

Bhaskara Rao, Digumarti, editor (2003). *Successful Schooling*. New Delhi: Discovery Publishing House. ISBN 81-7141-677-2.

Bhaskara Rao, Digumarti, editor (2003). *European Education and Teachers*. New Delhi: Discovery Publishing House. ISBN 81-7141-702-7.

Bhaskara Rao, Digumarti, editor (2003). *Teachers in a Changing World*. New Delhi: Discovery Publishing House. ISBN 81-7141-694-2.

Bhaskara Rao, Digumarti, editor (2004). *International Encyclopaedia of Learning to Live Together*, 4 volumes. New Delhi: Discovery Publishing House. ISBN 81-7141-848-1.

Vol. 1 *International Conference on Learning to Live Together.*

Vol. 2 *Globalization and Living Together.*

Vol. 3 *Curriculum for Learning to Live Together.*

Vol. 4 *Science Education for the Contemporary Society.*

Bhaskara Rao, Digumarti, editor (2004). *International Guidelines on Open and Distance Teacher Education*. New Delhi: Discovery Publishing House. ISBN 81-7141-777-9.

Bhaskara Rao, Digumarti, editor (2004). *Adult Learning in the 21st Century*. New Delhi: Discovery Publishing House. ISBN 81-7141-797-3.

Bhaskara Rao, Digumarti, editor (2004). *Educational Practices: Research and Recommendations*. New Delhi: Discovery Publishing House. ISBN 81-7141-835-X.

Bhaskara Rao, Digumarti, editor (2004). *General Secondary Education In the 21st Century*. New Delhi: Discovery Publishing House. ISBN 81-7141-885-6.

Bhaskara Rao, Digumarti, editor (2004). *Reforming Secondary Education*. New Delhi: Discovery Publishing House. ISBN 81-7141-843-0.

Bhaskara Rao, Digumarti, editor (2004). *Human Rights Education*. New Delhi: Discovery Publishing House. ISBN 81-7141-882-1.

Bhaskara Rao, Digumarti, editor (2004). *United Nations Decade for Human Rights Education*. New Delhi: Discovery Publishing House. ISBN 81-7141-887-2.

Bhaskara Rao, Digumarti and B.S.V. Dutt, editors (2003). *Education: Programmes and Policies*. New Delhi: APH Publishing Corporation. ISBN 81-7648-470-9.

Bhaskara Rao, Digumarti, C.A.P. Swamy and B.S.V. Dutt (1997). *Self-Evaluation in Student Teaching*. New Delhi: Discovery Publishing House. ISBN 81-7141-374-9.

Bhaskara Rao, Digumarti and D. Naresh Kumar (2004). *School Teacher Effectiveness*. New Delhi: Discovery Publishing House. ISBN 81-7141-782-5.

Bhaskara Rao, Digumarti and D. Sridhar (2002). *Job Satisfaction of School Teachers*. New Delhi: Discovery Publishing House. ISBN 81-7141-652-7.

Bhaskara Rao, Digumarti, C. Sridevi and K. Vijaya (1995). *Achievement in Social Studies*. New Delhi: Discovery Publishing House. ISBN 81-7141-281-5.

Bhaskara Rao, Digumarti and Digumarti Pushpa Latha (1994). *Achievement in Biology*. New Delhi: Discovery Publishing House. ISBN 81-7141-264-5.

Bhaskara Rao, Digumarti and Digumarti Pushpa Latha (1995). *Achievement in English*. New Delhi: Discovery Publishing House. ISBN 81-7141-283-1.

Bhaskara Rao, Digumarti and Digumarti Pushpa Latha (1994). *Achievement in Science*. New Delhi: Discovery Publishing House. ISBN 81-7141-280-70.

Bhaskara Rao, Digumarti and Digumarti Pushpa Latha (1995). *Achievement in Mathematics*. New Delhi: Discovery Publishing House. ISBN 81-7141-278-5.

Bhaskara Rao, Digumarti and Digumarti Pushpa Latha (2004). *Education for Women*. New Delhi: Discovery Publishing House. ISBN 81-7141-873-2.

Bhaskara Rao, Digumarti and Digumarti Pushpa Latha, editors (1998). *International Encyclopaedia of Women*, 5 volumes. New Delhi: Discovery Publishing House. ISBN 81-7141-410-9 (set).

Vol. 1 *Status of World's Women*. ISBN 81-7141-494-X.

Vol. 2 *Women, Education and Empowerment*. ISBN 81-7141-498-1.

Vol. 3 *Women Challenges and Advancement*. ISBN 81-7141-497-4.

Vol. 4 *Women and Family Health*. ISBN 81-7141-497-4.

Vol. 5 *Women and International Action*. ISBN 81-7141-498-2.

Bhaskara Rao, Digumarti, Digumarti Pushpa Latha and Digumarthi Harshitha, editors (2001). *Biological Warfare*. New Delhi: Discovery Publishing House. ISBN 81-7141-597-0.

Bhaskara Rao, Digumarti, Digumarti Pushpa Latha and Digumarthi Harshitha, editors (2001). *Women as Educators*. New Delhi: Discovery Publishing House. ISBN 81-7141-602-0.

Bhaskara Rao, Digumarti and Digumarthi Harshitha (2004). *Adjustment of Adolescents*. New Delhi: APH Publishing House. ISBN 81-7648-836-8.

Bhaskara Rao, Digumarti and Digumarthi Harshitha, editors (2001). *Education in India*. New Delhi: APH Publishing House. ISBN 81-7648-207-2.

Bhaskara Rao, Digumarti, Digumarti Pushpa Latha and Digumarthi Harshitha, editors (2001). *Assessing Learning Achievement*. New Delhi: Discovery Publishing House. ISBN 81-7141-601-2.

Bhaskara Rao, Digumarti, Digumarti Pushpa Latha and Digumarthi Harshitha, editors (2001). *Energy Security*. New Delhi: Discovery Publishing House. ISBN 81-7141-598-9.

Bhaskara Rao, Digumarti, Digumarthi Harshitha and K.R.S. Sambasiva Rao, editors (1999). *Advanced Biotechnology*. New Delhi: Discovery Publishing House. ISBN 81-7141-516-4.

Bhaskara Rao, Digumarti and K.R.S. Sambasiva Rao, editors (1996). *Current Trends in Indian Education*. New Delhi: Discovery Publishing House. ISBN 81-7141-311-0.

Bhaskara Rao, Digumarti and D. Naresh Kumar (2004). *School Teacher Effectiveness*. New Delhi: Discovery Publishing House. ISBN 81-7141-782-5.

Bhaskara Rao, Digumarti and E. Sreekanth Babu (2004). *Educational Interests of School Students*. New Delhi: Discovery Publishing House. ISBN 81-7141-837-6.

Bhaskara Rao, Digumarti and K. Vijaya (1995). *A Text Book Evaluation*. Ambala Cantt: The Associated Publishers.

Bhaskara Rao, Digumarti and M.A. Fayaz (2004). *Problems of Primary School Drop-outs*. New Delhi: Discovery Publishing House. ISBN 81-7141-834-1.

Bhaskara Rao, Digumarti and N.V.M. Mohana Rao (2002). *Problems of Mentally Handicapped Children*. New Delhi: Discovery Publishing House. ISBN 81-7141-645-4.

Bhaskara Rao, Digumarti and S. Chandra Mohan (2002). *Sports Management*. New Delhi: APH Publishing House. ISBN 81-7648-467-9.

Bhaskara Rao, Digumarti and S.A. Khader (2004). *Problems of Private School Teachers*. New Delhi: Discovery Publishing House. ISBN 81-7141-838-4.

Bhaskara Rao, Digumarti and S.A. Khader (2004). *School Education in India*. New Delhi: Discovery Publishing House. ISBN 81-7141-849-X.

Bhaskara Rao, Digumarti and S. K. Johni Basha (2004). *Teachers' Population Education Awareness*. New Delhi: Discovery Publishing House. ISBN 81-7141-832-5.

Bhaskara Rao, Digumarti, V.V. Rao, V.V. Lakshmi and V.V. Krishna, editors (1999). *Status and Advancement of Women*. New Delhi: APH Publishing Corporation. ISBN 81-7648-169-6.

Babu, P.C., author and Digumarti Bhaskara Rao, editor (2004). *Flowers of Wisdom*. New Delhi: Discovery Publishing House. ISBN 81-7141-695-0.

Amala, P.A. and Anupam, P., authors and Digumarti Bhaskara Rao, editor (2004). *History of Education*. New Delhi: Discovery Publishing House. ISBN 81-7141-860-0.

Bhagya Lakshmi, L., author and Digumarti Bhaskara Rao, editor (2000). *Reading and Comprehension*. New Delhi: Discovery Publishing House. ISBN 81-7141-543-1.

Bhasha, S.A., author and Digumarti Bhaskara Rao, editor (2004). *Methods of Teaching Geography*. New Delhi: Discovery Publishing House. ISBN 81-7141-807-4.

Bhuvaneswara Lakshmi, Gadde, author and Digumarti Bhaskara Rao, editor (2000). *Attitude Towards Science*. New Delhi: Discovery Publishing House. ISBN 81-7141-541-6.

Bhuvaneswari Lakshmi, G., author and Digumarti Bhaskara Rao, editor (2004). *Methods of Teaching Life Science*. New Delhi: Discovery Publishing House. ISBN 81-7141-804-X.

Bhuvaneswari Lakshmi, G. and K. Subba Rao, authors and Digumarti Bhaskara Rao, editor (2004). *Methods of Teaching Biology*. New Delhi: Discovery Publishing House. ISBN 81-7141-914-3.

Chowdary, S.B.J.R. and Naga Raju authors and Digumarti Bhaskara Rao, editor (2004). *Mastery of Teaching Skills*. New Delhi: Discovery Publishing House. ISBN 81-7141-861-9.

Devraj, T.A.S., author and Digumarti Bhaskara Rao, editor (1997). *Trace Analysis of Uranium and Thorium*. New Delhi: Discovery Publishing House. ISBN 81-7141-375-7.

Durga Rani, K., author and Digumarti Bhaskara Rao, editor (2000). *Educational Aspirations and Scientific Attitudes*. New Delhi: Discovery Publishing House. ISBN 81-7141-555-5.

Dutt, B.S.V. and Digumarti Bhaskara Rao (2001). *Empowering Primary Teachers*. New Delhi: Discovery Publishing House. ISBN 81-7141-615-2.

Dutt, B.S.V., author and Digumarti Bhaskara Rao, editor (2004). *Comparative Education*. New Delhi: Discovery Publishing House. ISBN 81-7141-912-7.

Ediger, Marlow and Digumarti Bhaskara Rao (1996). *Science Curriculum*. New Delhi: Discovery Publishing House. ISBN 81-7141-321-8.

Ediger, Marlow and Digumarti Bhaskara Rao (2000). *Teaching Mathematics Successfully*. New Delhi: Discovery Publishing House. ISBN 81-7141-552-0.

Ediger, Marlow and Digumarti Bhaskara Rao (2001). *Teaching Science Successfully*. New Delhi: Discovery Publishing House. ISBN 81-7141-600-4.

Ediger, Marlow and Digumarti Bhaskara Rao (2001). *Teaching Social Studies Successfully*. New Delhi: Discovery Publishing House. ISBN 81-7141-596-2.

Ediger, Marlow and Digumarti Bhaskara Rao (2002). *Philosophy and Curriculum*. New Delhi: Discovery Publishing House. ISBN 81-7141-631-4.

Ediger, Marlow and Digumarti Bhaskara Rao (2002). *Improving School Administration*. New Delhi: Discovery Publishing House. ISBN 81-7141-633-0.

Ediger, Marlow and Digumarti Bhaskara Rao (2002). *Elementary Curriculum*. New Delhi: Discovery Publishing House. ISBN 81-7141-658-6.

Ediger, Marlow and Digumarti Bhaskara Rao (2003). *Language Arts Curriculum*. New Delhi: Discovery Publishing House. ISBN 81-7141-657-8.

Ediger, Marlow and Digumarti Bhaskara Rao (2003). *Psychology and Curriculum*. New Delhi: Discovery Publishing House. ISBN 81-7141-691-8.

Ediger, Marlow and Digumarti Bhaskara Rao (2003). *Teaching Language Arts Successfully*. New Delhi: Discovery Publishing House. ISBN 81-7141-678-0.

Ediger, Marlow and Digumarti Bhaskara Rao (2003). *School Curriculum and Administration*. New Delhi: Discovery Publishing House. ISBN 81-7141-709-4.

Ediger, Marlow and Digumarti Bhaskara Rao (2003). *Teaching Mathematics in Elementary Schools*. New Delhi: Discovery Publishing House. ISBN 81-7141-687-X.

Ediger, Marlow and Digumarti Bhaskara Rao (2003). Teaching Science in Elementary Schools. New Delhi: Discovery Publishing House. ISBN 81-7141-698-5.

Ediger, Marlow and Digumarti Bhaskara Rao (2003). *School Curriculum and Administration*. New Delhi: Discovery Publishing House. ISBN 81-7141-709-4.

Ediger, Marlow and Digumarti Bhaskara Rao (2003). *Elementary Curriculum Improvement*. New Delhi: Discovery Publishing House. ISBN 81-7141-740-X.

Ediger, Marlow and Digumarti Bhaskara Rao (2004). *School Organisation*. New Delhi: Discovery Publishing House. ISBN 81-7141-843-0.

Ediger, Marlow and Digumarti Bhaskara Rao (2004). *Relevancy in Elementary Curriculum*. New Delhi: Discovery Publishing House. ISBN 81-7141-845-9.

Ediger, Marlow, B.S.V. Dutt and Digumarti Bhaskara Rao (2003). *Teaching English Successfully*. New Delhi: Discovery Publishing House. ISBN 81-7141-707-8.

Elizabeth, M.E.S., author and Digumarti Bhaskara Rao, editor (2004). *Methods of Teaching English*. New Delhi: Discovery Publishing House. ISBN 81-7141-809-0.

Harshitha, D. author and Digumarti Bhaskara Rao, editor (2004). *Methods of Teaching Information Technology*. New Delhi: Discovery Publishing House. ISBN 81-7141-805-8.

Indira Devi, author and J. Prasanth Kumar and Digumarti Bhaskara Rao, editors (2004). *Values in Language Text Books*. New Delhi: APH Publishing Corporation. ISBN 81-7141-833-3.

Jalaja Kumari, C., author and Digumarti Bhaskara Rao, editor (2004). *Methods of Teaching Educational Technology*. New Delhi: Discovery Publishing House. ISBN 81-7141-810-4.

Jayasree, Kandi, author and Digumarti Bhaskara Rao, editor (1999). *Correlates of Socialisation*. New Delhi: Discovery Publishing House. ISBN 81-7141-517-2.

Jayasree, Kandi, author and Digumarti Bhaskara Rao, editor (2004). *Methods of Teaching Science*. New Delhi: Discovery Publishing House. ISBN 81-7141-801-5.

John Babu, Chikati, author and T.J.R. Prasad, G.M. Madhukar and Digumarti Bhaskara Rao, editors (1996). *Problem Solving in Mathematics*. New Delhi: APH Publishing Corporation. ISBN 81-7648-273-0.

Joseph Raju, B and G.A. Anitha, authors and Digumarti Bhaskara Rao, editor (2004). *Population Education*. New Delhi: Sonali Publications. ISBN 81-88836-31-3.

Lalitha, T., author and K.S. Prabhakaram, D.S.N. Sastry and Digumarti Bhaskara Rao, editors (2004). *Educational Philosophic Beliefs*. New Delhi: Discovery Publishing House. ISBN 81-7141-765-5.

Madhu Bala, Jampala, author and Digumarti Bhaskara Rao, editor (2004). *Adjustment Problems of Hearing Impaired*. New Delhi: Discovery Publishing House. ISBN 81-7141-831-7.

Madhu Bala, Jampala, author and Digumarti Bhaskara Rao, editor (2004). *Methods of Teaching Exceptional Children*. New Delhi: Discovery Publishing House. ISBN 81-7141-802-3.

Marja, Talvi and Digumarti Bhaskara Rao, editors (1996). *Educational Leadership and Social Changes*. New Delhi: Discovery Publishing House. ISBN 81-7141-320-X.

Nageswara Rao, S.and M. Srihari, authors and Digumarti Bhaskara Rao, editor (2004). *Guidance and Counselling*. New Delhi: Discovery Publishing House. ISBN 81-7141-840-6.

Nageswara Rao, S. and P. Sridhar, authors and Digumarti Bhaskara Rao, editor (2004). *Methods and Techniques of Teaching*. New Delhi: Sonali Publications. ISBN 81-88836-33-8.

Nirmala Jyothi, M., author and Digumarti Bhaskara Rao, editor (2003). *Non-detention System in School Education*. New Delhi: Discovery Publishing House. ISBN 81-7141-654-3.

Padma Tulasi, G., author and Digumarti Bhaskara Rao, editor (2004). *Methods of Teaching Elementary Science*. New Delhi: Discovery Publishing House. ISBN 81-7141-871-6.

Pala Prasada Rao, V., author and K. Nirupa Rani and Digumarti Bhaskara Rao, editors (2004). *Methods of Teaching Elementary Science*. New Delhi: Discovery Publishing House. ISBN 81-7141-871-6.

Prabhakaram, K.S., author and Digumarti Bhaskara Rao, editors (1998). *Concept Attainment Model in Mathematics Teaching*. New Delhi: Discovery Publishing House. ISBN 81-7141-424-9.

Prasanth Kumar, J., author and Digumarti Bhaskara Rao, editor (1998). *Effectiveness of Distance Education System*. New Delhi: Discovery Publishing House. ISBN 81-7141-437-0.

Prasanth Kumar, J., author and Digumarti Bhaskara Rao, editor (2004). *Methods of Teaching Civics*. New Delhi: Discovery Publishing House. ISBN 81-7141-806-6.

Prasanth Kumar, J., author and G. Sundara Rao and Digumarti Bhaskara Rao, editors (2000). *Open University Student Support Services*. New Delhi: Discovery Publishing House. ISBN 81-7141-550-4.

Raja Kumari, M.A. and D.R.S. Sundari, authors and Digumarti Bhaskara Rao, editor (2004). *Special Education*. New Delhi: Discovery Publishing House. ISBN 81-7141-846-5.

Raja Kumari, M.A. and D.R.S. Sundari, authors and Digumarti Bhaskara Rao, editor (2004). *Methods of Teaching Educational Psychology*. New Delhi: Discovery Publishing House. ISBN 81-7141-820-1.

Ramatulasamma, K., author and Digumarti Bhaskara Rao, editor (2002). *Job Satisfaction of Teacher Educators*. New Delhi: Discovery Publishing House. ISBN 81-7141-655-1.

Rama Krishnaiah, D., author and Digumarti Bhaskara Rao, editor (1998). *Job Satisfaction of College Teachers*. New Delhi: Discovery Publishing House. ISBN 81-7141-438-9.

Rama Kumar Ratnam, M.V., author and Digumarti Bhaskara Rao, editor (1998). *Dukkha: Suffering in Early Buddhism*. New Delhi: Discovery Publishing House. ISBN 81-7141-653-5.

Rama Krishna Prasad and P. Vide Sagar, authors and Digumarti Bhaskara Rao, editor (2004). *Methods of Teaching Physical Education*. New Delhi: Discovery Publishing House. ISBN 81-7141-868-6.

Rama Seshaiah, P. author and Digumarti Bhaskara Rao, editor (2004). *Methods of Teaching Home Science*. New Delhi: Discovery Publishing House. ISBN 81-7141-916-X.

Ramesh, Ganta and Digumarti Bhaskara Rao, editors (1998). *Environmental Education: Problems and Prospects*. New Delhi: Discovery Publishing House. ISBN 81-7141-423-0.

Ranga Rao, R., author and Digumarti Bhaskara Rao, editor (2004). *Methods of Teacher Teaching*. New Delhi: Discovery Publishing House. ISBN 81-7141-812-0.

Rathaiah, Lavu and Digumarti Bhaskara Rao, editors (1996), *International Innovations in Education*. New Delhi: Discovery Publishing House. ISBN 81-7141-359-5.

Rathaiah, Lavu and Digumarti Bhaskara Rao (1997). *Achievement Correlates*. New Delhi: Discovery Publishing House. ISBN 81-7141-385-4.

Ravi Krishna, M., author and Digumarti Bhaskara Rao, editor (2004). *Examination System*. New Delhi: Discovery Publishing House. ISBN 81-7141-824-4.

Ravi Kumar, M., author and Digumarti Bhaskara Rao, editor (2004). *Methods of Teaching Computer Science*. New Delhi: Discovery Publishing House. ISBN 81-7141-823-6.

Reddy, Sudhakar Y., author and Digumarti Bhaskara Rao, editor (2003). *Creativity in Adolescents*. New Delhi: Discovery Publishing House. ISBN 81-7141-659-4.

Reddy, M. S., author and Digumarti Bhaskara Rao, editor (2004). *Creativity in College Students*. New Delhi: Discovery Publishing House. ISBN 81-7141-697-7.

Rudramamba, B., author and Digumarti Bhaskara Rao, editor (2003). *Problems of Teaching*. New Delhi: APH Publishing Corporation. ISBN 81-7648-462-8.

Rudramamba, B. and V. Lakshmi Kumari, authors and Digumarti Bhaskara Rao, editor (2004). *Methods of Teaching Economics*. New Delhi: Discovery Publishing House. ISBN 81-7141-900-3.

Sanjeeva Rao, P.C., author and Digumarti Bhaskara Rao, editor (1996). *A Text Book of Geology*. New Delhi: Discovery Publishing House. ISBN 81-7141-313-7.

Satya Narayana, V., author and Digumarti Bhaskara Rao, editor (2001). *Physical Education, Social Attitudes and Leadership Qualities*. New Delhi: Discovery Publishing House. ISBN 81-7141-593-8.

Satya Narayana, P.V.V. and G. Krishna, authors and Digumarti Bhaskara Rao, editor (2004). *Curriculum Development and Management*. New Delhi: Discovery Publishing House. ISBN 81-7141-813-9.

Siva Lakshmi, G.V. and G.L. Subbaiah, authors and Digumarti Bhaskara Rao, editor (2004). *Methods of Teaching Environmental Science*. New Delhi: Discovery Publishing House. ISBN 81-7141-839-2.

Srinivas, M. and I. Prasada Rao, authors and Digumarti Bhaskara Rao, editor (2004). *Methods of Teaching History*. New Delhi: Discovery Publishing House. ISBN 81-7141-803-1.

Srinivasulu Reddy, M. and K.R.S. Sambasiva Rao, authors and Digumarti Bhaskara Rao, editor (1999). *A Text Book of Aquaculture*. New Delhi: Discovery Publishing House. ISBN 81-7141-482-6.

Srinivasa Rao, Mandalapu, author and Digumarti Bhaskara Rao, editor (2003). *Achievement Motivation and Achievement in Mathematics*. New Delhi: Discovery Publishing House. ISBN 81-7141-674-8.

Sunil Kumar, K. and K. Rama Krishana, authors and Digumarti Bhaskara Rao, editor (2004). *Methods of Teaching Chemistry*. New Delhi: Discovery Publishing House. ISBN 81-7141-913-5.

Sunita, E. and R. Sambasiva Rao, authors and Digumarti Bhaskara Rao, editor (2004). *Methods of Teaching Mathematics*. New Delhi: Discovery Publishing House. ISBN 81-7141-915-1.

Swarupa Rani, T. and J.R. Priyadarshini, authors and Digumarti Bhaskara Rao, editor (2004). *Educational Measurement and Evaluation*. New Delhi: Discovery Publishing House. ISBN 81-7141-859-7.

Vanaja, M., author and Digumarti Bhaskara Rao, editor (1999). *Inquiry Training Model*. New Delhi: Discovery Publishing House. ISBN 81-7141-515-6.

Vanaja,M., author and Digumarti Bhaskara Rao, editor (2004). *Methods of Teaching Physics*. New Delhi: Discovery Publishing House. ISBN 81-7141-867-8

Valeri V. Koustiouk, author and Digumarti Bhaskara Rao, editor (2002). *A Text Book of Cryogenics*. New Delhi: Discovery Publishing House. ISBN 81-7141-642-X.

Vamsi Krishana, V., author and Digumarti Bhaskara Rao, editor (2004). *School Psychology*. New Delhi: Discovery Publishing House. ISBN 81-7141-880-5.

Veena Kumari, Balusu and Digumarti Bhaskara Rao (1996). *Operation Black Board*. New Delhi: APH Publishing Corporation. ISBN 81-7024-711-X.

Veena Kumari, B. author and Digumarti Bhaskara Rao, editor (2004). *Methods of Teaching Social Studies*. New Delhi: Discovery Publishing House. ISBN 81-7141-899-6.

Veena Kumari, Balusu, author and Digumarti Bhaskara Rao, editor (2000). *Psycho-Social Correlates of Achievement*. New Delhi: Discovery Publishing House. ISBN 81-7141-547-4.

Venkata Rao, P. and Digumarti Bhaskara Rao (1989). *A Text Book of Zoology—Junior Intermediate*. Guntur: Vignan Publishers.

Venkata Rao, P. and Digumarti Bhaskara Rao (1989). *A Text Book of Zoology—Senior Intermediate*. Guntur: Vignan Publishers.

Venkateswara Reddy, L. and Lakshmi Narayana, M., authors and Digumarti Bhaskara Rao, editor (2004). *Methods of Teaching Rural Sociology*. New Delhi: Discovery Publishing House. ISBN 81-7141-811-2.

Venkateswara Rao, V., author and Digumarti Bhaskara Rao, editor (2004). *Problems of Education*. New Delhi: Discovery Publishing House. ISBN 81-7141-841-4.

Venkateswara Rao, V., V. Vijaya Lakshmi and V. Vamsi Krishna, authors and Digumarti Bhaskara Rao, editor (2004). *Education For All*. New Delhi: Sonali Publications. ISBN 81-88836-30-3.

Venkateswara Rao, V., V. Vijaya Lakshmi and V. Vamsi Krishna, authors and Digumarti Bhaskara Rao, editor (2004). *Education in India*. New Delhi: Sonali Publications. ISBN 81-88836-858-9.

Venkateswara Reddy, L. and Lakshmi Narayana, M., authors and Digumarti Bhaskara Rao, editor (2004). *Education for Dalits*. New Delhi: Discovery Publishing House. ISBN 81-7141-872-4.

Venkateswarlu, K. and S.J. Basha, authors and Digumarti Bhaskara Rao, editor (2004). *Methods of Teaching Commerce*. New Delhi: Discovery Publishing House. ISBN 81-7141-808-2.

Venugopala Rao, K., author and Digumarti Bhaskara Rao, editor (2000). *Teacher Morale in Secondary Schools*. New Delhi: Discovery Publishing House. ISBN 81-7141-551-2.

Vidya, C., author and Digumarti Bhaskara Rao, editor (1996). *A Text Book of Nutrition*. New Delhi: Discovery Publishing House. ISBN 81-7141-309-9.

Vijaya Bharathi, D., author and Digumarti Bhaskara Rao, editor (2000). *Educational Philosophies of Swami Vivekananda and John Dewey*. New Delhi: APH Publishing House. ISBN 81-7648-309-9.

Vijaya Lakshmi, D., author and Digumarti Bhaskara Rao, editor (2004) *Basic Education*. New Delhi: Discovery Publishing House. ISBN 81-7141-881-3.

**Books in Telugu Language**

Bhaskara Rao, Digumarti (1986). *Dhrushya Sravana Bodhanapakaranalu (Audio Visual Teaching Aids)*. Guntur: Nagarjuna Publishers.

Bhaskara Rao, Digumarti (1993). *Jeevasashtra Bodhana (Teaching of Biology)*. Guntur: Nagarjuna Publishers.

Bhaskara Rao, Digumarti (1995). *Vignanasasthra Bodhana (Teaching of science)* Guntur: Nagarjuna Publishers.

Bhaskara Rao, Digumarti (1997). *Vidya Manovignana Seshtram (Educational Psychology)*. Guntur: Creative Press.

Bhaskara Rao, Digumarti (1998). *DSC Study Material*. Guntur: Nagarjuna Publishers.

Bhaskara Rao, Digumarti (1998). *Upadhyayudu Vidya. (Teacher and Education)* Guntur: Nagarjuna Publishers.

Bhaskara Rao, Digumarti (1998). *Vidya Drukpadalu (Perspectives of Education)*. Guntur: Nagarjuna Publishers.

Bhaskara Rao, Digumarti (1999). *EdCET Teaching Aptitude*. Guntur: Nagarjuna Publishers.

Bhaskara Rao, Digumarti (2001). *Bharata Samajamulo Upadyayudu Vidya (Teacher and Education in Emerging Indian Society)*. Guntur: Sri Nagarjuna Publishers.

Bhaskara Rao, Digumarti (2001). *Bhoutika Sastra Bodhana Paddathulu (Methods of Teaching Physical Science).* Guntur: Sri Nagarjuna Publishers.

Bhaskara Rao, Digumarti (2001). *Jeeva Sastra Bodhana Padhathulu (Methods of Teaching Biology).* Guntur: Sri Nagarjuna Publishers.

Bhaskara Rao, Digumarti (2001). *Vidya Manovignana Sastram (Educational Psychology).* Guntur: Sri Nagarjuna Publishers.

Bhaskara Rao, Digumarti (2003). *Patasala Yajamanyam / Paripalana (School Management and Administration).* Guntur: Sri Nagarjuna Publishers.

Gopala Krishna, G., A. Ramkrishna, K. Subba Rao and Bhaskara Rao, Digumarti (2004). *Jeevasashtra Bodhana Padhatulu (Methods of Teaching of Biological Science).* Guntur: Sri Nagarjuna Publishers.

Krishna Murthy, V., K.S. Sudheer Reddy and Digumarti Bhaskara Rao (2004). *Vidya Manovignana Sastra Adharalu (Foundations of Educational Psychology).* Guntur: Sri Nagarjuna Publishers.

Lalini, V., V. Dayakara Reddy, M. Srihari and Digumarti Bhaskara Rao (2004). *Vidya Adharalu (Foundations of Education).* Guntur: Sri Nagarjuna Publishers.

Subba Rao, K.P., P. Ayodhya and Digumarti Bhaskara Rao (2004). *Patasala Yajamanyam-Vidhya Vyavasthalu (School Management and Systems of Education).* Guntur: Sri Nagarjuna Publishers.

Sudhakar, V., B. Ravindra Babu, D.S. Kumar and Digumarti Bhaskara Rao (2004). *Vidya Sanketika Sastram-Computer Vidya (Educational Technology and Computer Education).* Guntur: Sri Nagarjuna Publishers.

# Index

## D



## E

## H



## I

## R



## S